SITUATION VACANT

The Social Consequences of Unemployment in a Welsh Town

by Joe Miller

Afterword by Community Projects Foundation

Author's Note

This report was commissioned by the Community Projects Foundation (CPF) in February 1981. It has been financed by CPF, Newport Borough Council and the Julian Melchett Trust.

Many people have helped me with information and ideas over the last six months:

- representatives of 50 local organisations have been interviewed;

- visits were made to Edinburgh, Glasgow, Hamilton, London, Paisley, Port Glasgow, Shotton, Sheffield and St. Helens in order to see at first hand a variety of community and industrial development projects;

- those researching in this field were contacted and I visited Glen Massey who is studying workers made redundant from the East Moors Steel Works, and Chris Harris from Swansea University who is undertaking a major study of those made redundant from the BSC Steelworks at Port Talbot;

- a door to door survey was carried out on two estates in Newport, resulting in information on 307 households and 701 adults. There was an overall response rate of 84%.

- the libraries are now flowing with new material about unemployment and I have read as much as I could.

Special thanks are due to members of South Gwent Community Aid, the steering group for the research; John Dainton and Mike Fell of Newport Borough Council; to many kind and helpful people at BSC Llanwern; to Steve Clarke, Trevor Davidson, Steve Dowrick, Phil Gibbs, Rex Hewitt, Cathy Jarrold, Julie O'Donaghue, Wendy Sammons and especially Ray Taylor.

I was given enormous help in the preparation and analysis of the door to door survey by Martin Read of the Sociological Research Unit, University College, Cardiff. The survey simply would not have been completed without his skill and hard work.

The errors and inadequacies of the report are mine.

Joe Miller
October 1981

Contents

List of Tables

Introduction

Situation Vacant is a study of some important aspects of the local economy and of the social consequences of economic stress in Newport. Clearly, there are close links between fluctuations in the economy and personal and social well-being. And in Newport the distressing consequences of economic change and unemployment are widespread and deep.

The aim of the report is to provide an up-to-date analysis of unemployment and its consequences in Newport, as a basis for thinking about possible ways to remedy the situation and regenerate the economic and social basis of local life.

In carrying out this study we have produced a picture of a town and its people which we believe may well be of much wider interest since the events now affecting Newport are repeated in towns and cities all over Britain.

The evidence for our picture comes both from existing sources and from a survey conducted specifically for the purpose of this report. Over 300 households in Bettws and Ringland (84% of our attempted sample) answered questions about their employment situation and its effects on their lives. We refer to this as the Newport People and Jobs Survey 1981.

In our survey, over 21% of the people we interviewed were currently unemployed; 30% of them had been unemployed at some time in the last two years; and 45% of households had experience of unemployment in that period. At the same time, 35% of those in full-time employment felt insecure or very insecure about their future prospects. And full-time housewives suffered anxieties and health effects quite as severe as the unemployed. Large numbers of people in a variety of positions are therefore affected.

Much of the data for the study was collected in Bettws and Ringland and so, although randomly sampled and typical of many areas, the results cannot be generalised to the whole town. Nonetheless, the survey provides a valuable insight into what life is like now for significant numbers of people in Newport.

What then is to be done? The problems in South Wales have developed over a long period. Over the years inward investment has been encouraged through regional policies in order to mitigate the worst effects of job losses in traditional industries. Nationalised industries and the relocation of government offices have been especially important in providing direct employment. Indeed, Humphreys described South Wales as 'the closest thing to a nationalised region that exists in the country'.[1]

In Newport in 1975 the top 13 employers accounted for 44% of total jobs in the town: 36% of the working population were employed in local and central government bodies. Only 9% of firms were under some form of local control. Five of the top employers were private companies, and they accounted for 8% of total employment in the town. None of the five were locally controlled and, only two were British companies, which together provided about 2% of employment in the town.

Regional policies have resulted in the formation of large organisations, generally branches of central government or multi-national companies. This leaves local communities vulnerable to a wide variety of changes quite outside their control. The benefit of inward investment has therefore to be put alongside the drawbacks. The danger always is that one set of lost dependencies are replaced by another.

Some of these economic pressures are being combatted through the encouragement of small-scale, diverse companies and services, publicly and privately controlled, and locally based, preferably locally generated. It is this aspect of the local economy which now needs greater impetus.

People feel defeated and hopeless. Local action to regenerate economic and social life is urgently needed. In the final section I have suggested some broad directions for this which I hope will be helpful in formulating policy.

We need to recognise though that not enough jobs will be created, indeed unemployment will increase and it will remain high. New social enterprises are therefore also needed in order to compensate for the reduction in employment opportunities. This is probably our most daunting and perplexing challenge. It is one which calls for the greatest degree of self-help and new imaginative thinking on the part of local organisations.

I can only hope that this report will be a useful aid in the development of thinking, and that this will lead to effective action.

---

1. G. Humphreys (1972), Industrial South Wales Newton Abbot: David & Charles

CHAPTER ONE

EMPLOYMENT AND UNEMPLOYMENT

Employment

i The Industrial Character of Newport

Newport probably first became significant because its ports coincided with a crossing point on the River Usk - that was in the fifth century. By 1521 it was described as:

> 'a burgh and a proper town and hath goodly haven coming into it....whereunto very great ships may resort and have good harbour'.[1]

Just over 400 years later, in 1958, the town acknowledged the long-lasting power of its geographical position by adopting the motto, 'Terra marique' - 'By land and sea'. There is a strength in this position which transcends fashion: and it is the fundamental characteristic upon which the town's future so greatly depends.

The modern world too relies on good communications. Newport Docks and the town's location at the intersection of important road and rail links are attractive to industrial and commercial developers. Trunk roads link with motorways to the Midlands and the North; the M4 now crosses almost the entire length of industrial South Wales; whilst to the east the Severn Bridge has made London and the South East an easy drive. This is complemented by intercity train services making Heathrow airport readily accessible. If Gwent is the gateway to Wales, then Newport is its keeper. There is no regular wage for the post, but it has nonetheless proved to be a most rewarding position!

In 1801 its population was about 1100. By the end of the century this had reached 70,000. The town had become a centre for the distribution of the rich coal and iron deposits of the valleys. Now, though still crucially important, the metal industries are employing fewer workers, and in their stead the newer micro-electronics companies are being wooed by the same combination of natural advantages, although grant aid and political pressures naturally play their part as well.

The population has, of course, continued to grow throughout the century and some recent figures are provided in Table 1.

There have been fluctuations. A rise between 1951 and 1971, due largely to the development of the Llanwern Steelworks and its associated housing schemes, has now been reversed. Since 1971 there has been a net loss due to migration.

---

1. In a survey of the estates of the Duke of Buckingham

Migration, of course, usually involves the young members of the community, so the future population structure is affected. It also involves a diminution of the skilled workforce.

In the years to 1971 the national increase in the birth rate was exceeded in Newport. For example, in 1971 the 0-4 year age group in the town represented 8.7% of the population, compared with 8.4% in Gwent and 8% in Great Britain. The bulge has already passed through the schools and into the working population. There are therefore now large numbers of young workers. There is also a decreased number of older workers and a corresponding increase of those moving into retirement.

Table 1: Population

	1951	1971	1981
Newport	122,400	136,847	133,698
Gwent	404,700	441,379	439,684
Wales	2,598,700	2,731,200	2,790,000
Great Britain	48,854,300	53,978,500	54,128,000

Source: Census 1981: Preliminary Report, HMSO

Some idea of the working population is given in Table 2. The areas are those as defined and used by the County Council.

Table 2: Employed in Gwent

	1959	1975
Upper Valleys	32,100	28,500
Lower Valleys	19,000	18,400
Eastern Valley	32,200	38,900
Coast (predominantly Newport)	66,100	75,500
North East	7,500	12,200
Gwent	156,900	173,500

Source: Gwent County Council

Newport is by far the largest employment centre in the county. In 1971 the town provided 68,000 jobs: 19,000 people (28%) travelled to it each day for work: and only 14% commuted out - the lowest figure in the county.

The town centre alone provided 11,000 jobs in shops, distributive, administrative and professional services, and it had become a regional shopping centre and the principal town of the county.

ii The Shift from Manufacturing to Services

But the coal and steel industries, upon which the local economy has depended, are now providing fewer and fewer jobs. There has been a fundamental shift from manufacturing to services. Table 3 shows the process very clearly: from 1966 to 1976 there was a 24% reduction in jobs in manufacturing in the town and at the same time a 22% increase in jobs in services. By 1976, 55.6% of the working population in Newport was employed in services.

Table 3: Employment Sectors: Newport

	Newport Employment Exchange Area			Great Britain
	Numbers Employed 1966	1976	% change 1966-76	% change 1966-76
Primary & Extractive	429	322	- 24.9	- 30.8
Manufacturing	32,722	24,933	- 23.8	- 21.5
Services	29,436	35,890	+ 21.9	- 5.6
Total	68,259	64,589	- 5.4	- 6.4

Source: Census of Employment
Newport Borough Industrial and Employment Monitor, July 1980

In 1980, in Great Britain as a whole, a further 0.5 million jobs were lost in manufacturing and 140,000 added in services.

Table 4: Employment Sectors: Great Britain

	Manufacturing	Services	All
September 1979	6,995,000	12,980,000	22,295,000
September 1980	6,455,000	12,840,000	21,550,000

Source: MSC Review, March 1981

It was during this period that Newport was experiencing heavy redundancies in manufacturing. Furthermore, the growth that has occurred has been largely for female workers. In Gwent in 1959 women formed 25% of all employees; by 1975 this had risen to 36%, with the greatest growth in Newport.

Table 5: Male and Female employees in Gwent: changes 1959-75			
	Male	Female	Total change
Upper Valleys	- 6,500	+ 2,900	- 3,600
Lower Valleys	- 5,200	+ 4,600	- 600
Eastern Valley	- 400	+ 7,100	+ 6,700
Coast (predominantly Newport	+ 4,600	+ 4,800	+ 9,400
North East	+ 1,500	+ 3,200	+ 4,700
Gwent	- 6,000	+22,600	+16,600

Source: Gwent County Council

The 4,600 increase in jobs shown for men in the coastal district was due to the development of the Llanwern Steelworks; without this there would have been a loss of 1,400 jobs between 1959 and 1966.

iii Concentration of Employment

By the 1980s Newport's employment base had become dangerously narrow, depending upon metal manufacturing, distributive and scientific and professional services. But employment was also concentrated in a relatively small number of organisations and firms. Since the recent BSC redundancies, the vulnerability of this position neeeds no underlining.

This concentration of employment is shown in Table 6.

In 1976 these major employers provided 28,400 jobs, 44% of total employment in the town, with those having 1,000 or more workers accounting for 39% of jobs.

A closer look reveals that 23,000 of these jobs, a little under 36% of total employment in Newport, were in local or central government bodies. Only about a quarter of these were under some form of local control. In other words, although these major governmental organisations accounted for 36% of the jobs in Newport, only about 9% were locally controlled.

Table 6: Major employers (firms with 500+ employees) in Newport, 1976	
Employer	Estimated number of employees
British Steel Corporation	12,500
Gwent Area Health Authority	3,500
Alcan Booth	1,900
Newport Borough Council	1,900
British Rail	1,500
Standard Telephone Company	1,400
GPO	1,300
Department of Trade & Industry	1,100
Monsanto	800
CEGB	700
Crompton Parkinson	700
British Transport Docks Board	600
IMI Santon	500

Source: Employment Census
Newport Borough Council

Far fewer jobs, 5,300, were located in major privately owned companies. This represented 8% of total jobs in the town. None of these firms are locally controlled as Table 7 shows.

Table 7: Major private employers in Newport showing parent company		
	Parent Company	Location of Parent Company
Alcan Booth	Alcan Aluminium (UK Ltd). a subsidiary of Alcan Aluminium Ltd.	Canada
Standard Telephone Co.	International Telephone & Telegraph Corporation	USA
Mansanto Ltd.	Monsanto Co.	USA
Crompton Parkinson	Hawker Siddeley Group Ltd.	UK
IMI Santo	IMI Ltd.	UK

Source: Who Owns Whom: UK. 1981 published by Dun & Bradstreet Ltd.

A little additional mathematics reveals that of the 5,300 employees working in these major private firms, 4,100 were in three companies controlled from the USA or Canada.

The two British companies, Crompton Parkinson and IMI Santon, together provided 1,200 jobs in the town, a little under 2% of total employment. But these companies are both multi-national corporations with world-wide interests. This trend towards a concentration of ownership is further evidenced in Table 8.

Table 8: Proportion of manufacturing output produced by top 100 companies in Great Britain

	% of output in top 100 companies
1950	20%
1970	50%
1985*	66.5%

* Estimate provided by the National Institute of Economic Research

Source: 'The State and the Local Economy', CDP Political Economy Collective, Newcastle upon Tyne. 1979.

These facts and figures clearly illustrate the relatively narrow base of the local economy and its dependency upon relatively few employers.

This dependency has worried local authorities, but the balance of local ownership is unlikely to change in the short term. It has been estimated that over 14,000 jobs will be needed in Newport to get unemployment down to 3.5% by 1991 (Newport Borough Council, Industrial and Employment Monitor, July 1980). And the source of these new jobs was clearly laid down in Gwent County Council's Structure Plan Report, 1978:

> "Fundamentally new employment opportunities for the Gwent workforce must be 'imported' from both other parts of the United Kingdom and from abroad."

This aim has underpinned industrial development policy before and since. It was reinforced in June 1980 when the Newport travel-to-work area was upgraded to Development Area status and later when the Welsh Development Agency was empowered to spend £48m in the Newport and Port Talbot areas.

iv The Wider Context: Technology and Employment

The facts about Newport need also to be seen in the context of more general contemporary questions about the meaning of employment. Both world recession and the particular problem of Britain in the 1980's force us to ask whether it is any longer sensible to think of a society in which the majority will be employed?

Our economic ills can be partly explained by the following factors: oil price rises, world recession, a massive increase in the world's population - doubling before the end of the century - and Britain's difficulty in competing because its manufacturing base is out of date, badly managed and overmanned.

Every industry in the following table illustrates a further trend and one which has been strengthened in more recent years - the replacement of labour with capital.

Table 9: Investment and employment: Increase in gross capital stock and in plant and machinery from 1963-76, compared with employment figures in the same industries

Industry	Increase in Gross Capital Stock at Constant Replacement Cost	Increase in Plant and Machinery at Constant Replacement Cost	Employment: Increase/ Decrease
Agriculture forestry and fishing	56%	24%	- 43.5%
Mining & quarrying	69%	35%	- 49.2%
Food, drink & tobacco	70%	90%	- 9.8%
Coal & petroleum products, chemical & allied industries	69%	81%	- 4.0%
Other metals, engineering & allied industries	38%	39%	- 8.9%
Bricks, pottery, glass and cement	81%	93%	- 18.4%
Timber, furniture etc.	71%	88%	- 5.5%
Paper, printing and publishing	50%	57%	- 10.4%
Construction	114%	146%	- 18.2%
Gas, electricity & water	58%	65%	(gas) - 20.6% (e&w) - 14.3%

Source: MSC Review and Plan, 1977

Now minds concentrate on the consequences of the staggering developments in micro-electronics. The tiny, energetic micro-processor is being applied in more and more everyday devices and machines. The overall loss of jobs is already significant: ICI can run a synthetic plant on a few staff: Metra International say that in the current 5 years to 1983, office jobs will decline by 50%. Almost everyone has a story to tell of how new technical equipment is doing work that was once considered to be highly skilled, as well as the more mundane, repetitive tasks.

How are these jobs to be replaced? The micro-processor was not developed to increase employment, quite the reverse. And although new technologies can be harnessed for useful social purposes, this will not increase the numbers of jobs available to people. Or are people expected not to work?

Today a person's identity is inextricably bound up in work. When people are asked what they do, they reply with a description of their employment. It is man's closest tie to reality, according to Freud. Thus the disturbing effects of unemployment - and we shall examine these in some detail - make a world without employment very difficult indeed to envisage.

One of the leading researchers concerning the social consequences of unemployment, Professor Marie Jahoda, writes:

> 'We ourselves have formed the impression that the human needs met by....employment are relatively enduring and that, therefore, unemployment now will have disturbing psychological consequences similar to those documented during the great depression....unless alternative social arrangements provide an acceptable rational purpose that produces the categories of experience human beings appear to need.'
>
> M. Jahoda and Howard Rush, 1980, Work, Employment and Unemployment, Science Policy Research Unit, University of Sussex. p.52

Many argue that as technological developments displace large numbers of people, alternatives to paid employment must be developed or there will be personal and social breakdown on a quite massive scale. J.L. Gershony, argues that the 'hidden economy', if properly developed, could well provide part of the answer. It sometimes sounds like a sort of underground liberation movement: but at present the 'hidden economy' probably represents a relatively small proportion of total output. Sir William Pile, head of Inland Revenue Services estimates it to be 7%.

Whatever the solution may be, the problem is not simply one of creating jobs, but of seeking out new forms of work that will be satisfying for people and which are needed by society. Without the latter, there are justifiable fears that we shall simply find tasks to fill people's time: something which can only result in alienation and frustration.

We need to maximise capacities within the local economy to generate jobs, and also to maximise the search for satisfying work in order to compensate for an economy that will not automatically generate jobs for large numbers of people. Some thoughts and pointers for policies and practices to meet these needs are put forward in the final part of the report.

Unemployment

i Official Unemployment Statistics and Survey Figures

Tables in this section provide official unemployment figures for 1970, 1980 and 1981. Between June 1977 and June 1981 unemployment in Newport rose by 4,411, or 103%, and most of that increase, 3,275, or 74%, occurred between 1980 and 1981. In Table 10 figures are provided for June/July 1981 wherever possible because this was the time during which we conducted the door to door survey. Unemployment has continued to rise since and in September 1981 it stood at 9,406, or 14.9% of the travel to work area.

In the survey we conducted, 21.3% of the economically active in Bettws and Ringland were currently unemployed. The official register for the Newport Travel-to-Work area was a little over 13.6% at the time when the survey was completed. This difference can be explained mainly by the fact that these two areas are likely to contain larger numbers of unemployed people than Newport as a whole. However, part of the explanation is that not all of the unemployed register is seeking employment with the Job Centre or Careers Office. This is fully dealt with in the next chapter.

In the survey we also discovered that:

- 30% of the economically active had been unemployed at some point in the last 2 years.

- 45% of households had experience of unemployment in the last 2 years through at least one of its members.

- 6% of individuals had never had a job.

In other words, unemployment, although affecting 13.6% overall, according to official data for June 1981, affects some areas more than others and many more people and households over a period of time.

Table 10: Official unemployment statistics and survey figures

PLACE	MALES Job Centre	MALES Careers Office	FEMALES Job Centre	FEMALES Careers Office	TOTAL	PERCENTAGE M	PERCENTAGE F	PERCENTAGE T
JUNE 1979								
NEWPORT	2,721	200	1,126	270	4,317			
Remainder of Travel-to-Work Area	786	127	470	117	1,500			
					5,817	6.8	6.2	6.6
Gwent	8,324	896	3,793	1,052	14,065	7.9	7.4	7.7
Wales	49,858	4,249	21,787	4,138	80,032	8.1	6.2	7.3
Great Britain	887,211		394,891		1,282,102	6.3	4.1	5.4
JUNE 1980								
NEWPORT	3,342	288	1,485	287	5,402			
Remainder of Travel to Work Area	1,009	127	627	161	1,924			
					7,326	8.4	7.7	8.1
Gwent	10,070	1,060	4,913	1,180	17,223	9.7	9.2	9.5
Wales	61,188	5,458	27,294	5,127	99,067	10.1	7.4	9.0
Great Britain	1,082,933		503,712		1,586,645	7.8	5.2	6.7
JUNE 1981								
NEWPORT	6,209	319	1,920	229	8,677			
Remainder of Travel to Work Area	2,173	186	968	187	3,514			
					12,191	15.6	7.7	13.6
Gwent	17,513	1,377	6,776	1,175	26,841	16.2	11.7	14.6
Wales	107,080		42,372		150,352	16.3	10.1	13.9
Great Britain	1,844,904		732,240		2,577,144	13.3	7.6	10.9

Source: Employment Gazette, HMSO

ii Registration of Unemployed

The official unemployment figures are a count of those registered as unemployed and available for work on a particular day of the month.

A number of people who want work do not register, however; they may not be entitled to claim benefit, this is especially true of married women who opt not to pay the full national insurance contributions. It is also true of some young people, the retired and those whose claims are disallowed. But married women appear to be the major group involved. In late 1977 the Department of Employment estimated an undercount of women at 150,000 to 200,000.

* The 1971 Census recorded 1.4 million as unemployed and yet the officially registered for that month was 0.8 million: a difference of 75%.

* The 1978 General Household Survey said that of those seeking work, 20% were not registered.

* In our survey, we asked detailed questions of one member of the household, 27% of these were seeking work, but not registered. When the whole household is included this figure for unregistered job seekers rises to a little over 29%.

Table 11: Under - registration of unemployed

	Registered	Unregistered
1971 Census	57%	43%
1978 General Household Survey	80%	20%
1981 'People and Jobs' Survey	73%	27%

17% of those not registered were men and 83% women. The age range for women was broad, although rather more younger women were seeking work. Most unregistered men were in their late 40s.

The 1981 edition of <u>Social Trends</u>, published by The Central Statistical Office, estimated that 75% of the unregistered unemployed were women, and that over half of them were seeking part-time work.

We asked housewives if they would take a job if the opportunity arose. 41.4% of them said that they would, but only 24% of these were registered: 76% were not.

The overwhelming number of housewives who wanted jobs (88%) needed work in order to supplement the family income. And the major reasons for not being able to work were children (44.1%), health (14.7%) and age (14.7%).

This is most important. A large number of people are available for work and will take jobs if the opportunity arises: many of them are women. For example, in January 1981 there were 10,000 enquiries and 8,000 applications for 300 vacancies at the new Asda store in Swansea: total registered unemployed in the Swansea Valley at that time was 13,000. Obviously many people who were not registered as seeking work applied for these jobs, and although some of these will have current jobs, many do not.

The local workforce is therefore enormously influenced by the unregistered unemployed. And their needs, if left unsatisfied, will nevertheless still affect its functioning.

There are at least two further important factors which must be taken into account when assessing unemployment.

iii Short-time Working

At the end of 1980, 509,500 people in Great Britain were supported by the Temporary Short-time Working Compensation Scheme (MSC March 1981). That represents about 2.4% of the total of those in employment.

In our survey 4.1% of those in full-time work were on short-time working at the time of being interviewed. Additionally, in any one of the previous four weeks between 6.2% and 7.4% worked for under 34 hours per week.

On the other hand, over 77% of the respondents worked 40 or more hours and nearly 24% worked more than 45 hours.

The vast majority of part-time workers, about 60%, worked between 10 and 20 hours per week.

iv Government Schemes

At the end of 1980, 257,500 people in Great Britain, about 1.2% of total employees, were on other temporary government schemes.

In 1971 the under 20s unemployed was 76,000, just over 11% of the total. By 1979 there were 268,300 unemployed young people on average, representing nearly 22% of the total. And, according to the Manpower Services Commission, youth unemployment is likely to 'double or even treble over the next few years'. (MSC Review. March 1981)

In June 1981, 800 young people in Newport were on temporary schemes which takes the total for that month without permanent work to 1,348. By August 1981 the totals had reached 1,226 (33.3%) and 2,425 (67.4%) respectively.

v Who is Unemployed?

It is often thought that the unemployed are a single, unchanging, amorphous group. This is untrue, of course. In our survey, we discovered that 30% of the economically active had been unemployed at some point in the last two years. But who is unemployed and for how long? Let us look first at the ages of those who have been unemployed.

Table 12: Unemployed in Newport: Ages

Age	Percentage of that age group
16 - 19 years	66.7%
20 - 34 years	43.4%
35 - 49 years	20.6%
50 - 64 years	21.8%

Source: Newport People and Jobs Survey 1981

This clearly indicates that the young are more likely to experience unemployment, and the likelihood of unemployment decreases with age. When we look at the recurrence of periods of unemployment, again the young show through as being most likely to be unemployed on more than one occasion. And the only people who were unemployed on three or more occasions were aged under 20 years.

Table 13: Unemployed in Newport in the last two years: Number of times unemployed and ages

No. of times unemployed	%	% age group			
	Overall	16-19	20-34	35-49	50-64
Once	80.6	37.5	79.4	89.5	100%
Twice	18.1	50.0	20.6	10.5	-
Three times	1.4	12.5	-	-	-

Source: Newport People and Jobs Survey 1981

People are also staying out of work for longer periods.

Table 14: Length of Unemployment: Great Britain		
	January 1980	January 1981
	000s	
0 - 3 months	570	879
0 - 6 months	276	552
6 - 9 months	141	301
9 - 12 months	83	159
over 12 months	334	430

Source: MSC Review, March 1981

One of the questions in our survey sought to discover how long it was before people were going back into work. The time periods do not coincide with those above, but they do indicate the strengthening of the trend towards longer periods of unemployment.

Table 15: Length of unemployment: Newport	
Back in work within:	Percentage of total
2½ months	20%
5 months	34%
1 year	61%
2 years	80%

Source: Newport People and Jobs Survey, 1981

According to W.W. Daniel[1], 90% of the unemployed returned to work within one year in 1975. In our survey this percentage was not reached by the end of the second year.

Daniel suggests that long-term unemployment is underestimated by one-third because unemployment is interrupted by sickness. This is probably now becoming less marked as the Department of Employment continue to pay unemployment benefits to those temporarily sick.

But if the general trend is towards longer periods of unemployment, precisely who remains unemployed longest? The following is an analysis of the January 1981 unemployment figures for Newport - the calculations are approximate; it is extremely difficult to work out accurate figures for duration of unemployment by age group.

---

1. W.W. Daniel, Why is unemployment still somehow acceptable? (New Society, 19th March 1981.)

Table 16: Duration of unemployment: Official Statistics: January 1981						
Total unemployed	3	6	MONTHS 12	12+	24+	36+
7,911	1,114 14%	2,285 29%	3,000 38%	896 11%	383 5%	233 3%
Percentages are of the total unemployed						

Source: Newport Industrial and Employment Monitor

In other words, in January 1981, 7,911 people were unemployed: 14% for 3 months, 29% for 6 months, 38% for 12 months, 11% for between 1 and 2 years, 5% for between 2 and 3 years, and 3% for over 3 years.

If we take two of these periods, let us say the period between 6-12 months and the period 12 months to 2 years, and analyse by age group, the following result emerges.

Table 17: Unemployed 6-12 months by age				
Total	Under 20	20-34	35-49	50+
3,000	558 44.5%	1,241 39%	549 35.5%	656 35%
Percentages above are of that particular age group				

Table 18: Unemployed for over 12 months by age				
Total	Under 20	20-34	35-49	50+
896	35 3%	392 12%	201 13%	268 14%
Percentages are of that particular age group				

Source: Newport Industrial and Employment Monitor

There are significantly higher proportions of younger people unemployed for periods of up to twelve months and significantly higher proportions of older people for periods of over twelve months. Higher numbers were recorded for those aged between 60-64 years. In Great Britain over 25% in this age group are unemployed for more than 2 years. (Social Trends, 1981)

These trends were confirmed by our survey. 19% of those who had been unemployed in the last two years had been so for between one and two years; 20% for more than 2 years. No person under 20 had been unemployed for over one year: but larger numbers were recorded for under one year. Generally, we recorded higher percentages for all age groups of those unemployed for over one year and correspondingly lower percentages for periods of unemployment under one year compared with the January figures for Newport as a whole.

vi Mismatch

A comparison of socio-economic groupings adds a further perspective to the plight of the unemployed.

Table 19: Economically active or retired: social-economic Groups by head of household

	Employers + Managerial	Profes- sional	Non Manual	Skil- led	Semi- skilled	Un- skilled	Armed Forces + others
Blaenau Gwent	5.7	1.2	11.1	45.7	16.9	10.9	8.5
Islwyn	7.4	1.6	11.7	47.5	17.5	8.5	5.8
Monmouth	15.6	4.5	17.2	31.2	16.0	5.6	9.9
Torfaen	8.0	3.1	14.5	36.9	21.0	9.5	7.0
Newport	9.7	3.9	15.7	37.9	14.9	11.4	6.5
Gwent	9.3	2.9	14.0	39.8	17.3	9.2	7.5
Wales	11.9	3.9	13.8	42.8	15.4	8.0	4.2

Source: 1971 Census, 10% Sample

In Newport there were relatively fewer skilled and relatively more unskilled in the local workforce in 1971. There are however relatively few vacancies for unskilled people. The mismatch between people and job opportunities is then aggravated because certain skills and experience are no longer relevant: massive structural changes are generating a process in which people are being de-skilled.

For example, the following table, which matches the skills of the unemployed against vacancies, shows that there were only 55 vacancies for the 3,161 unskilled people on the register at that time: and only 30 vacancies for the 745 skilled engineers.

Table 20: Skills of unemployed matched against vacancies: Newport Job Centre				
	Registered Unemployed Dec. 1980	Vacancies Handled Sept-Oct 1980	Registered Unemployed March 1981	Vacancies Handled Dec. 1980-Feb. 1981
Building Trades - skilled	503	95	638	54
Skilled Engineering Trades	667	64	745	30
Hotel and Catering	263	132	267	140
Miscell. skilled + semi-skilled	1,165	235	1,248	264
Clerical	788	92	852	425
Commercial	508	235	542	182
Admin, Profess ional + Executive	152	61	179	63
Unskilled	3,033	69	3,161	55
	7,079	983	7,632	1,214

Source: Newport Job Centre
Newport Borough Council

The chances of anyone finding work are therefore deteriorating. This includes young people who have been on a government assisted scheme.

Table 21: Young people finding work after YOP schemes in Newport: Percentages			
	Number Leaving Schemes	Number Entering Permanent Work	Percentages
June 1979	174	87	50.00%
June 1980	130	62	47.49%
June 1981	323	111	34.27%

Source: County Careers Office

The Department of Applied Economics at Bangor University estimated that in 1974 7 out of every 10 young people in Wales got jobs after such schemes, but in June 1981 this had fallen to 3 in 10.

vii Job Seeking

The most persistent job seekers are still younger people, but Table 22 may indicate a loss of hope in that relatively large numbers are now not applying for jobs.

Table 22: Seeking work and the number of jobs applied for	
Number of jobs applied for:	Percentage of unemployed
none	26%
1 - 5	35%
6 - 10	9%
11 - 15	11%
16 - 20	9%
21+	9%
Don't know	1%

Source: Newport People and Jobs Survey 1981

But even if 26% of our sample had not applied for a job, 35% had applied for up to 5 jobs and 38% had applied for more than 5 jobs.

For how long did people believe they would be unemployed?

Table 23: Expectations of length of unemployment	
Return to work period	Percentage of unemployed
Within 1 month	11%
Within 3 months	6.5%
Within 6 months	10%
Within 1 year	3%
When the economy picks up	18%
Never have another job	11%
Don't know	40.5%

Source: Newport People and Jobs Survey, 1981

These perceptions related to some extent to previous experience, those who had experience of brief periods of unemployment thought that they would soon return to work. But the vast majority were resigned to lengthy periods of unemployment.

Who were those who thought that they would never work again?

It is astonishing that 14% of the unemployed under 20s we interviewed thought that they would never work again. But the under 20s do get back into work and far fewer than 43% of those aged 35-49 years remain unemployed. We must therefore take these perceptions more as a measure of their despair than as a realistic judgement of their chances of remaining unemployed.

Table 24: 'Never work again' by age groups

	Percentage of those who thought they would never work again
16 - 19 years	14%
20 - 34 years	nil
35 - 49 years	43%
50 - 64 years	29%
65+	14%

Source: Newport People and Jobs Survey 1981

The basic implication of this analysis is that programmes related to the unemployed should not think of them as a single undifferentiated group, but one which contains quite different sorts of people. Although large numbers of people are in despair about their future prospects, most of the unemployed still do see themselves as 'seeking work' and would not respond in significant numbers to social programmes purely related to the unemployed. Indeed, programmes for unemployed people must clearly recognise that they should appeal to many different people in very many different ways.

viii Redundancies

The motivation behind this study was the imminent redundancies from the Llanwern Steelworks. But less than 1 in 5 redundancies are of this classic, large-scale type; less than 1 in 10 of those made redundant receive more than £500; only 1 in 25 receive £2,000 or more, and these are generally older people.

In the years before the major Llanwern redundancies, between 1976 and 1980, there were 11,157 notified redundancies in Newport. The majority were in metal manufacturing, but large numbers were also recorded in the construction industry and the remainder were widely spread.

The Manpower Services Commission estimate that notified redundancies can be increased by 15% because they only account for redundancies where 10 or more workers are involved. On this basis, redundancies in Great Britain for 1980 could be increased from 390,000 to 448,500: and those in Newport between 1976 and 1980 could have amounted to 12,800 people.

Table 25: Major redundancies 1976-80: Newport

Metal manufacturing	5,445
Construction	3,289
Electrical Engineering	627
Distributive trades	347
Textiles	231
Transport	226
Total	10,165

Sources: Department of Employment
Newport Borough Council

Some important facts about redundancy emerged from our survey:

- 13% of our sample had been made redundant at some point in the last two years

- the under 20s are more likely to be made redundant than other age groups: 30% of those aged under 20 had been made redundant

- the highest numbers of redundancies were in the 20-34 age group and the 35-49 group, each accounting for 35% of all redundancies

- the vast majority of those made redundant go into unemployment, only 3% went directly to another job

- about 37.5% of all those made redundant did get a job subsequently

- data concerning our main respondents, from whom we obtained detailed information, show that of those made redundant in the last two years, nearly 62% were still unemployed when we interviewed them, 21% were in employment and 7% described themselves as housewives.

A breakdown of redundancies in Gwent for 1980 reveals a further worry, as appears in Table 26.

The breakdown should focus interest on the figure of 950 redundancies in service industries, an increase of 700 on 1979. This indicates that such industries cannot continue to offset job losses elsewhere in the present economic circumstances.

Table 26: Major redundancies in Gwent: 1980		
	Redundancies	% of total
Steel	4,853	43%
Other manufacturing	4,370	39%
Services	950	8%

Source: Gwent County Council

ix Llanwern Redundancies

At an early stage in this study it was thought that it would be about the Llanwern redundancies, but however important these are, they really do form only part of the current picture about unemployment in the town. Nevertheless, they are central and command more considered attention than other redundancies.

There have been three phases of redundancy from the Llanwern Steelworks:

October 1979		409	redundancies
June/Sept 1980	'Slimline 1'	3,766	"
March 1981	'Slimline 2'	232	"

Most of what follows concerns the impact in Newport of the major redundancy phase: Slimline 1. The table which follows shows that 59% of those made redundant from Llanwern live in Newport - roughly the same proportion of Newport residents as in the total Llanwern workforce.

Table 27: Llanwern redundancies: Place of residence	
Place	Percentage of workforce made redundant
Newport Borough	59%
Monmouth District	13%
Islwyn Borough	11%
Torfaen Borough	10%
Remainder of adjoining areas	5%

Source: Newport Borough Council, Employment Monitor, October 1980

I have estimated the distribution within Newport and Caerleon of workers actually made redundant from the steelworks. The estimate was made by taking a 20% random sample of addresses of workers who left Llanwern in 1980. These addresses were then allocated to areas and the major concentrations are shown in Table 28.

Table 28: Llanwern redundancies: Residence within Newport: Major concentrations*		
	Numbers	Percentage of Newport Total
Ringland	255	12.6
Alway	143	7.0
Liswerry	138	6.8
Llanmartin/Underwood	138	6.8
Malpas	132	6.5
Bettws	127	6.3
Caerleon	117	5.8
St. Julians	97	4.8
Maindee	82	4.0
Somerton	76	3.8
Barnardtown	56	2.8
Lawrence Hill	46	2.3

* Note: The numbers include some workers who left BSC who were not part of the redundancy programme.

Source: British Steel Corporation

In reality, most of these areas merge so, for example, the total in the Ringland, Alway, Liswerry and Somerton area is 612.

Therefore redundancies were concentrated on Newport, and within Newport some areas contain high proportions of steelworkers.

What do we know about those who were made redundant? Table 29 provides some of the picture.

This list is not completely accurate because many changes occurred at the last minute, after the list was produced, but it clearly indicates the trend:

- over 46% are 45 years or more

- nearly 44% of those were process workers

- of the 54% aged under 45 years, over 62% were process workers

- about 22% were aged 55+

The majority of those made redundant were therefore at a positive disadvantage in obtaining further work.

What has happened to these people? Until December 1980 a detailed record was kept by the Manpower Services

Commission; it is in Table 30.

Table 29: Llanwern Redundancies: Age and occupation of Newport residents											
Age Range: Job	Under 20	20-24	25-29	30-34	35-39	40-44	45-49	50-54	55-59	over 59	Total
Process Worker	31	140	111	114	94	91	101	85	109	67	943
Technican		7	1	5	5	4	2	-	3	2	29
Fitter		7	12	9	11	5	8	10	9	7	78
Electrician		5	5	6	5	7	15	17	11	6	77
Boiler maker		7	7	2	8	4	7	14	14	10	73
Carpenter		2	-	2	-	2	4	1	1	2	14
Bricklayer		-	1	-	1	2	3	2	1	2	12
Maintenance - semi-skilled		25	25	20	21	20	34	38	62	12	257
Clerical - non supervisory	7	11	7	4	7	7	4	10	15	3	75
Supervisory staff		3	2	9	13	15	17	36	20	9	124
Management		-	2	8	10	5	5	13	16	3	62
	38	207	173	179	175	162	200	226	261	123	1,744
Grand total:	1,744										

Source: Newport Borough Council

After December 1980 only a record of those remaining unemployed was kept. This is shown in Table 31. This record was discontinued as from June 1981.

These records provide a good deal of information:

- the number of those unemployed has fallen from the high level of 1,889 in October 1980 until in May 1981 it was 1,358: 6% of these were females. In June the numbers registered as unemployed in Newport went up again to the March total. There was an increase of 15 men and 28 women. No explanation can be offered for this: it could be an accounting error. This is only a record of those who registered and stayed on the register. If a person leaves the register, for however short a period of time, or goes on a TOPS course and subsequently becomes unemployed, that person does not reappear in subsequent records;

- up to December 1980, 774 people were submitted for jobs by the Job Centre of whom 82 were placed;

- of the 323 who left the register between October and December 1980 only 44 were placed by the Job Centre, clearly indicating that most people still find work in their own ways.

The majority of the registered unemployed live in Newport, the remainder are widely distributed.

Table 30: Llanwern Redundancies: Employment Status, July - December 1980

	July 1980	August 1980	September 1980	October 1980	November 1980	December 1980
Workers Terminated	361	2,364	3,231	3,493	3,529	3,545
Advance Registrations	1,727	2,596	2,631	2,631	2,631	2,631
Subsequent Registrations	39	144	746	942	1,003	1,018
Submissions	250	412	504	621	707	774
Placings	5	19	38	62	72	82
Registrants known to have found work	-	4	28	105	231	249
Registered as unemployed	33	269	1,740	2,019	1,782	1,696
Applications for training	141	301	329	330	347	352
Allocated to a training course	1	6	14	81	225	242

Source: Manpower Services Commission

Table 31: Llanwern Redundancies: Registered unemployed

	January 1981	February 1981	March 1981	April 1981	May 1981	June 1981
Newport Job Centre	899	866	804	784	759	802
Other areas total	739	693	709	652	599	574
Total	1,638	1,559	1,513	1,436	1,358	1,376

Source: Manpower Services Commission

Figures obtained from the British Steel Corporation for the 30th May 1981 differ in two respects from those supplied by the MSC. The BSC figures indicate that there are more unemployed, 1,411 as opposed to 1,358, and more on training courses, 430 as opposed to 352. But apart from the discrepancies, the figures do throw further light on the position of those made redundant.

Table 32: Llanwern Redundancies (May 1980): Registered unemployed by area

Place	Number	Percentage of total
Newport	759	56.0%
Chepstow	167	12.0%
Risca	127	9.5%
Cwmbran	75	5.5%
Remainder of Gwent	131	9.5%
Adjoining Areas	49	3.5%
Registered with PER	50	4.0%

Source: Manpower Services Commission

Table 33: Llanwern Redundancies: Make-up pay[1]

Unemployed: 55 years + and on make-up pay	577
Unemployed: 55 years and under - not on make up pay	834
In employment on make-up pay	1,017
Undergoing training on make-up pay	430
Total:	2,858

Sources: British Steel Corporation
European Coal and Steel Community

Table 33 shows the number of workers who are on make-up pay. Make-up pay lasts for 52 weeks at 90% of the total wage and 26 weeks at 80% of the total wage.

One of the most significant aspects of large scale redundancies has been that those made redundant have tended to get jobs at the expense of the longer term unemployed. Make-up pay has exacerbated this. It has made low paid jobs more attractive to the redundant worker and there are cases where lower pay has been offered by employers precisely because it will be 'made up' from public funds. These low paid jobs are the very ones normally done by the long-term unemployed.

But what happens when the make-up pay phase ends? The same question can be asked of those on training. What then? At this time, unless there is a major improvement in the economy, the living standards and well-being of large numbers of workers will deteriorate.

The DHSS office in Newport has yet to see many claimants from Llanwern redundancies, but there is concern at the widespread misunderstanding that redundant workers

1. On the 4th September there were 660 people aged 55+ who were unemployed, and 890 unemployed and under 55 years not on make-up pay: there was an increase to 1,201 in employment and on make-up pay and a decrease to 374 on training courses and on make-up pay.

who simply spend until they have below £2,000 can then readily claim benefits. This is not the case. They must show that they did not deliberately spend to below that figure! This indicates one further possible aspect of future difficulty and embarrassment.

But none of this tells us how many workers are doing jobs with which they are dissatisfied. Nor does it tell us how many have left unsatisfactory jobs to go to another or to become unemployed. The trend has always been that workers made redundant from established enterprises often do get jobs, but that many are dissatisfied when they conpare them with their previous position: large numbers then move on. Precisely what the position is in Newport is impossible to say: the sort of information required is simply not available for the Llanwern redundancies.

CHAPTER TWO

SOCIAL CONSEQUENCES

Financial Consequences

i Household Finance

In our survey we asked a number of questions about household finance. Firstly, we asked everyone about their ability to balance the household budget.

Table 34: Household finance: survey results			
	It is not possible to make ends meet	We can just make ends meet	We manage quite well at the moment
Overall result			
Households in each category: total sample	16%	60%	24%
Breakdown of overall result			
Households with children	18%	60%	22%
Households without children	14%	59%	27%
Households with:			
Single adult	17%	57%	26%
Adults	13%	71%	16%
Households where main respondent:			
Full-time worker	6%	59%	35%
Unemployed	30%	63%	6%
Households where main respondent:			
Unemployed in last 2 years	27%	60%	13%
In work in last 2 years	12%	60%	28%

Source: Newport People and Jobs Survey, 1981

16% of households are unable to pay their way. Single adults, families with children and the unemployed are more likely to find themselves in this position than others, although there is little difference in the actual numbers in this category of those who had been in work throughout the last two years and those who had been unemployed at some time.

60% of households could just make ends meet. We recorded similar proportions of households with and without children and the numbers of children in the household tended not to affect the position. There were, though, more households in this category where there was more than one adult, although the position did not change as the numbers of adults increased.

24% of households could manage well. Generally, they were families without children, and single adult households where the respondent was in full-time work and had been so throughout the previous 2 year period.

Within the whole community, those aged between 20-49 years were most hard pressed, although the position varied predictably with socio-economic groupings. Also, the more changes in employment status, the greater the chances of running into financial difficulties.

ii Income in and out of work

Let us look a little more closely at what happens to a person's income during periods of unemployment.

According to the MSC, average incomes drop by 35% during periods of unemployment. Robert Taylor, the Observer's Labour Correspondent, calculated a drop of 46% (Observer, 1st March 1981).

This fall in income alone will have serious implications for the individual and the community: spending power is reduced, options for activity close in, and self-esteem is damaged. Most social agencies see the root of problems in this loss of spending power. And in Newport it should be remembered that at present people made redundant from Llanwern are still earning make-up pay. As training courses end, as length in unemployment increases, as redundancy money runs out, so increasing numbers are returning to the Llanwern counselling service for help: and what will happen when the eighteen month long make-up pay periods come to an end?

But what is the position of those in work? Here too the plight of those on low incomes must be taken into account. The Low Pay Unit's recent report[1] claims that 4.7 million workers in full-time employment and 2.8 million in part-time employment earn less than £75 per week, the Unit's definition of low pay. Most rely on overtime: and so in a time of depression they will be squeezed even tighter. The lowest 10% are worse off still; their pay has gone down compared with their position three years ago, where as the top 10% are relatively better off. The most vul-

---

1. March 1981, Low Pay Unit, London.

nerable are in industries in decline, such as steel; in the public sector, for example hospitals; and in industries which are inadequately unionized, such as agriculture.

Table 35: Individual income in and out of work for representative family types

Marital Status	Sex	Dependents	Gross Weekly Earnings	Net Disposable Income in work	Disposable weekly income out of work	Income out of work as a percentage of income in work
Single	Female	None	£56.00	£44.78	£28.34	63%
Single	Male	None	£90.50	£65.17	£28.34	43%
Married	Male	Wife	£90.50	£67.61	£39.95	57%
Married	Male	Wife + 2 children	£90.50	£77.79	£57.26	74%
Married	Male	Wife + 4 children	£90.50	£94.71	£82.51	87%

Notes:

(1) Gross weekly earnings set at three-quarters of national average levels.

(2) Table relates to persons becoming unemployed April 1980.

(3) Out of work income is for those unemployed between 29 and 52 weeks

(4) Calculations assume full claims made for: child benefit, rent + rate rebates, free school meals and welfare milk.

(5) No account taken of work expenses saved or perquisites lost when unemployed.

Source: Review of Services for the Unemployed: March 1981, Manpower Services Commission

Adrian Sinfield[2] claims that there is a growing 'social distance' between those in and those out of work, the relatively better off and the relatively poor. This is self-evident from discussions with those in and out of work. One professional woman in Newport spoke to us of her feelings of guilt at being untouched by the current recession. And I have noticed some surprise in others when I suggest how difficult a time many people are having.

For the low paid family every increase of £1 in earnings is wholly or substantially offset by reductions in means

2. Adrian Sinfield, 1981, What Unemployment Means, Martin Robertson, Oxford.

tested benefits[3]. People earning between £41-£59 per week suffer through increased earnings. It is not until £80 per week that a family will gain more than 50p per week for each extra £1 earned. Let us look at some characteristics of the 'poverty trap' as it is called:

- income tax begins at £42 per week
- Family Income Supplement and school meals end at £60 per week
- free school meals end at £76 per week
- rent rebates end at £85 per week
- rate rebates end at £92 per week.

At the end of 1979 the DHSS estimated the following:

- 50,000 families with children would receive no increase from £1 rise in income
- a further 60,000 families with children and 10,000 without children would receive less than 25p from a £1 rise in income
- a further 150,000 families with children and 100,000 families without children would receive between only 25p - 49p for the £1 rise.

iii Benefits and Entitlements

We were particularly interested in the extent of dependency on social security. In 1979 three million adults in Great Britain were receiving supplementary benefits: if their dependents are added, a total of five million people benefitted. In addition, about one-fifth of pensioners receive supplementary benefits. Social security represents an increasing proportion of average income: 4.9% in 1969 and 7.1% in 1979, in part reflecting the increased numbers of elderly and unemployed in the community.

We asked people whether anyone in the household was receiving any of the major benefits and entitlements which we listed on a card and showed them. Table 36 sets out some of our results.

---

3. <u>Social Trends 1981</u>, Central Statistical Office, HMSO

Table 36: Benefit and Entitlement: Make-up	
Benefit	**Recipients**
Retired people:	Percentage of those entitled:
State retirement pension	100%
Private or company pension	64%
Households with children:	
Child or Family Allowance	94%
Family Income Supplement	1.3%
Benefits	Percentage of total sample
Supplementary	24%
Rent Rebate/Allowance	20%
Rate Rebate	14%
Unemployment Benefit	14%
Attendance Allowance	nil
Mobility Allowance	0.3%
No benefits or entitlements	15%

Source: Newport People and Jobs Survey, 1981

The DHSS office in Newport estimate that there are 6,000 supplementary pensioners in the area, 3,000 - 4,000 claimants on short-term benefits, and 8,000 - 9,000 other claimants of which about half are unemployed. The number of supplementary benefit claims does increase with unemployment. But the DHSS maintain that the numbers of deliberately unemployed and other fraudulent claimants are very small indeed.

In our survey 58% of the under 20s were claiming supplementary benefits, the proportion decreases to 26% for the 20-34 age group and continues to decrease until retirement. 50% of the retired people in our sample were claiming this benefit. 24% of families with children were claiming, with no significant difference with increases in the number of children.

During the period 1974 to 1979 the real value of unemployment benefit was 'more or less' maintained, according to Social Trends, 1981. This is also true of supplementary benefits. But recent changes in government policy have militated against this. The local DHSS office confirms that benefits are not now keeping pace with inflation.

It is worth noting that although a very small proportion (1.3% of families with dependent children) are claiming Family Income Supplement (FIS), this is about at the national average.

Who is not claiming any benefit or entitlement?

Table 37: Not claiming benefits and entitlements	
Employment status	% within that category
In full-time work	32.5%
In part-time work	19.0%
Others	5.0%

Source: Newport People and Jobs Survey, 1981

These overall figures demonstrate the widespread dependency there is on benefits and entitlements. Over two-thirds of those in full-time work are claiming something and over 80% of those in part-time work: the proportion shoots to 95% for all other people. But it is necessary to be far more precise.

Within the working population dependency decreases with age (the under 40s containing most claimants), employment in full-time work, and households without dependent children. Conversely, there is a high incidence of dependency amongst the retired, lone adults, unemployed people and households with children. Beneficiaries are not of course confined to these categories. Also the take-up of many benefits is said by Government departments to be well below the potential.

iv Household Expenditure

We asked people what they spent their money on and whether they were having to cut down on or eliminate some item of expenditure. Table 38 sets out the overall results.

The essentials are going up in price. The DHSS office in Newport have noticed a dramatic increase in debt, especially fuel debts, over recent months: this is partly because bills come in at quarterly intervals and people have been unable to save the required amount. Some luxuries are being cut out completely. However, although a holiday and other forms of relaxation can be thought of as a luxury, they obviously provide a release from daily stress. Without it, the burden is obviously that much greater.

Unemployed people increase expenditure on essentials less than the employed and greater numbers reduce expenditure wherever possible. A larger percentage of the unemployed (59%) are not going to save this year compared with the employed (48%). Similarly, many more of the unemployed are going without a holiday, 54%, as opposed to 40% of those in full-time work.

Table 38: Household expenditure: Survey Results				
	Spending compared with the same time last year*			
Item of expenditure	More	Less	Same	No Expenditure
Food and Housekeeping	83%	6%	6%	-
Fuel (e.g. electricity and gas)	82%	3%	9%	-
Clothing & Footwear for the children	64%	8%	16%	1
Clothing & Footwear for adults	31%	23%	25%	13%
Drinks	21%	19%	13.5%	40%
Tobacco	34%	16%	16%	22%
Things for the home (furnishings & appliances)	21%	14%	12%	43%
Savings	3%	16%	14%	58%
Holidays	12%	15.5%	16%	47%
Leisure and Entertainment	15%	23%	22%	31%
Transport (fares & petrol)	53%	10%	17%	9%
Incidentals for children	49%	14%	21.	4%

* I have omitted the relatively small numbers who said that they were unsure.

Source: Newport People and Jobs Survey, 1981

Let us extract some of the more interesting detail.

Households having to increase expenditure on:

- food and housekeeping 83%
- fuel 82%
- clothing and footwear for children: 64%
- transport: 53%

Households not spending anything on:

- savings: 58%
- holidays: 47%
- things for the home: 43%
- drinks: 40%
- leisure and entertainment: 31%

v Impact on Local Spending

The impact of reduction in individual incomes on the commercial life of the town is severe and serious. In June 1981 we asked a number of businesses about the effects of them:

* Marks and Spencer reported that their Newport shop had dropped some 4% behind the sales volume of others.

* Tesco's, Newport's largest shop, was £50,000 per week down on sales.

* Travel Agents reported that people were economising on holidays, buying budget holidays, going later and going self-catering.

* Cinema attendances were down. One Manager reported an overall reduction in spending.

* Night clubs and working men's clubs reported drastic reductions in attendances. Once inside the club, spending per head was also down. A similar picture was reported by most of the publicans we spoke to. Reductions of 50% in sales was common.

* Council rent arrears have increased over a long period and there are many causes. However the local economic situation has made matters worse. In the private sector, mortgage repayments have been maintained. Building Societies demand only the repayment of interest during periods of unemployment. If people do get into difficulties, they are advised to move to a smaller property.

* Activity at the cheaper end of the housing market is buoyant, but houses costing more than £20,000 are difficult to sell. Fewer people are moving: that costs £2,000 in itself. If people do want to move outside the town, this is difficult unless their firms help. At the same time, there has been what one estate agent described as 'a downward surge' in the number of people wanting to move into Newport.

One young man described how he had developed a stomach ulcer, partly because he was worried about his future employment, but in particular because of the long drawn out problem he had experienced in selling his house.

vi Local and Central Government Income

So far we have looked at the loss of income suffered by individuals and households and its commercial impact.

But there is also a cost to government. 2.5 million unemployed people costs the Government £7,405 million in lost revenue and the country £10,76 billion in lost production, (MSC Review, March 1981).

Table 39: Loss of Revenue to Government		
Revenue	Married man with two children on average wage	Single man on average wage
Income Tax	£1,328	£1,547
Indirect Tax	400	531
Employee NI Contributions	434	434
Employers NI Contributions	887	887
Total Revenue Loss	£3,049	£3,399
Cost of Benefits		
Flat Rate Unemployment Benefit	£1,734	£ 960
Other Benefits	1,223	1,336
Total cost of benefits	£2,957	£1,837
TOTAL FINANCIAL COST	£6,006	£5,236

Source: House of Lords Hansard, November 12 1980
Written answer to Lord Kilmarnock Col 1454

Local government is similarly affected at a time when it is having to spend more to combat unemployment. One local authority, Strathclyde, has estimated that it spends £57 million (1980) as a direct consequence of unemployment.

Crime

Is this lack of money already leading to social problems? Is it leading, for example, to an increase in crime?

People travel into Newport in large numbers in order to work, shop and to be entertained; it is also the largest town in Gwent. It is therefore not surprising that between 60% and 65% of all police work in Gwent is concentrated in the Newport Division - an area roughly coinciding with the Newport Borough boundaries.

Up to the early part of 1981 there was no upturn in crime, but recently thefts related to electricity meters and shoplifting have increased. No figures are available, however, and some increase could be an increase in detection rates rather than acutual thefts.

For example, Marks and Spencer do not report an increase in shop-lifting; but because Tesco's have employed more store detectives, they may be catching more thieves - they have reported an increase.

An underlying trend has been the increase in the number of warrants issued by the police. These increased by 1,000 between 1979 and 1980, but in the current year this figure had already been reached by June.

This is partly explained by the fact that fewer custodial sentences are being passed - people are therefore fined. Now these fines are not being paid: and the categories of offences for which the fines were imposed are becoming more extensive, i.e. more people and a greater cross-section are unable to pay fines.

A disturbing national trend towards more elderly people being prosecuted for shoplifting may also be reflected in Newport, though there is no hard factual evidence as yet. It may also be that the amateur is being caught in what is an increasingly vigilant atmosphere.

The link between unemployment and the elderly is not obvious, but this is something to look into more closely. All the OAP clubs suggested that both increasing concern for young families, often resulting in financial outlay, were putting the elderly under greater financial pressures. This is confirmed by the Newport DHSS office where a spokesman agreed that more elderly people were becoming claimants because they had found themselves in difficulties.

Health

i Health and Unemployment

The first person to show clearly the historical relationship between the functioning of the economy and the health of a nation was Thomas McKeown in his book, The Modern Rise of Population, published by Edward Arnold in 1977. In that book he identifies improving health with improving wealth, and the claim of medicine to have been a major factor in the increase in population is proved false. Most medical advances followed long after death rates from disease had effectively declined.

Currently, a leading researcher in this field is an American professor from John Hopkins University, Harvey Brenner. He relates the well-being of the economy to the well-being of the individual.

Using complex statistical techniques, Brenner tries to correlate certain economic indicators: employment, per capita income and inflation, with certain pathological indicators: overall mortality, mortality from cardio-vascular disease and cirrhosis of the liver; suicide and hospitalisation of the mentally ill; imprisonment, and homicide. The methods used are complex and controversial because different time lags are computed as the various conditions show themselves after different intervals of time have elapsed.

One major finding[1] was that a 1% increase in unemployment sustained over 6 years in the USA had been associated with approximately 36,887 extra deaths, including 920 extra suicides and 648 extra murders, and also 4,227 extra state mental hospital admissions.

Brenner was asked to do a small-scale study in Britain for Granada Television's World in Action in 1980. He said that between 1972 and 1977, 300 deaths in Nottingham could be attributed to unemployment; at the same time, in Liverpool a 1% increase in unemployment probably led to 220 deaths; and that in Great Britain, between 1950 and 1975 a 1% increase in unemployment led to a 2.1% increase in mortality - 17,000 deaths.

A Welsh office report[2] estimates that if Wales experiences only one-twentieth of UK results predicted on the basis of Brenner's approach[3], the consequences in five years of the increase of 50,000 unemployed in Wales over the last 3 years could be:

- 2,500 extra deaths
- including 35 extra suicides
- 6 or 7 extra murders
- 3,195 admissions to mental hospitals
- 695 extra prison sentences

But we should be cautious: the methods used are under critical scrutiny at the moment, and detailed conclusions

---

1. M.H. Brenner 1976 'Estimating the Social Costs of National Economic Policy: Implications for Mental and Physical Health and Criminal Aggression' Joint Economic Committee, Congress of the United States. US Government Printing Office, Washington DC.

2. 'The Implications of Rising Unemployment for Personal Social Services in Wales'. Joint Working Party of Directors of Social Services and the Welsh Office. March 1981.

3. B. Rowthorn and T. Ward 'How to run a company and run down an economy: the effects of closing down steel-making in Corby.' Cambridge Journal of Economics, 3, 1979.

must be treated with circumspection. At the same time, though, we should recognise that what is being proposed is not so startlingly new as first appears: work has always affected health, it always has been a primary cause of physical and mental illness. Similarly, the absence of work with its consequential loss of income and increased psychological pressure has also always been a cause of illness. And severe changes within the economy have always resulted in more dramatic changes in health. The current interest in the subject is deepening our understanding of the complexity of these relationships.

What then are the major stress factors during periods of economic difficulties which are cited as giving rise to ill health?

- anxiety about loss of jobs
- depletion of resources and loss or reduction of income
- difficulties in planning ahead
- moving between jobs causes stress and financial loss
- loss of status, both when having to take a lower paid or more menial job, and when unemployed
- emotional upheaval sustained over a long period

Prolonged stress is a prime cause of ill health because it can damage the body's immune and cardiovascular systems.

> 'The former can lead to a reduction in the body's ability to fight off infections or malignant diseases, whilst the latter involves large fluctuations in factors such as blood pressure, cholesterol levels and the blood's tendency to clot. All these are associated with an increased risk of heart disease. Stress can also lead to an increase in health damaging behaviour, such as smoking, drinking and over-eating.'
>
> Jennie Popay, 'Unemployment: A Threat to Public Health'[1]

ii The Employed and Job Security

Our survey showed that these stress factors are present throughout the community: in those with work as well as those without - although the poor are always hardest hit

---

1. Chapter 5 in a forthcoming book: Unemployment: Who Pays the Price? 1981, Child Poverty Action Group.

by bad health.[2] The Daily Telegraph on the 18th September 1980 reported a Gallup poll which showed that the proportion of people who thought their own job was at risk had risen from 27% to 38% between June and September 1980.

Our own survey sheds more light on this. Tables 40 and 41 indicate the level of security about their jobs felt by those in employment.

Table 40: People in Employment: Feelings of job security

	All	In full-time employment	In part-time employment
Very secure	21%	22%	18%
Fairly secure	24%	25%	24%
Secure	20%	18.5%	22%
Insecure	24%	21%	29%
Very insecure	11%	13.5%	7%

Source: Newport People and Jobs Survey, 1981

35% of the working population feel insecure or very insecure. Deep insecurity was concentrated in the young. No-one over the age of 45 felt very insecure. And no-one over the age of 54 said they felt insecure. A high level of job insecurity was reported for the 40-49 year old age group: 37% of those aged 40-44 and 42% of those aged 45-49 said they felt insecure.

Table 41: People in Employment: Feelings of security by age group

Age	Very secure	Fairly secure	Secure	Insecure	Very insecure
16-24	31%	23%	8%	15%	23%
25-34	25%	12.5%	25%	16.5%	21%
35-44	16%	29%	13%	29%	13%
45-54	22%	25%	22%	31%	-
55-64	25%	33.5%	33.5%	8%	-

Source: Newport People and Jobs Survey, 1981

iii Levels of Anxiety: Everybody

We have some means from our survey to compare levels of anxiety throughout the community. We asked all of our

2. See for example the General Household Survey, 1975, 1976 1978 Office of Population Census and Surveys, HMSO.

respondents to tell us how worried they felt about the jobs situation in Newport.

Table 42: Worry about the jobs situation	
	Total Respondents
Very worried indeed	35%
Fairly worried	36%
Not worried	29%

Source: Newport People and Jobs Survey, 1981

71% of the total population in our sample felt worried: 35% were very concerned. We do not have other studies with which to compare this data, but at first sight it does appear to indicate a high level of anxiety amongst the general population.

We can delve a little into this. Firstly, does the experience of unemployment affect levels of anxiety?

Table 43: Worry about the jobs situation and employment record in the last 2 years		
	Unemployed at least once in the last 2 years	Fully employed during the last 2 years
Very worried indeed	52%	32%
Fairly worried	38%	38%
Not worried	10%	30%

Source: Newport People and Jobs Survey, 1981

The extremes are affected: those who have personally experienced recent unemployment are more likely to be very anxious and unlikely to be unworried, compared with the employed.

But because the numbers of employed are greater than the unemployed, there is a higher proportion of very worried workers in the total population (22%) than unemployed people (15.5%). The middle range is similar for both groups and there is a much larger number of unworried workers (30%) than unemployed people (10.5%).

Let us take a look at anxiety levels in some major groups other than the unemployed.

We are beginning to see that although anxiety is spread throughout the community, its impact varies in relation to particular groups. Table 44 tells us that relatively more housewives are affected and the following table indicates that overall anxiety levels decrease with age.

Table 44: Anxiety: groups other than the unemployed			
	% within category		
	very worried indeed	fairly worried	not worried
Those in work	30%	38%	32%
Full-time housewives	33%	44%	23%
Retired	19%	23%	58%

Source: Newport People and Jobs Survey, 1981

Table 45: Levels of anxiety and age - % within each group					
	16-19	20-34	35-39	50-64	65+
Very worried indeed	50%	36%	41%	31%	16%
Fairly worried	33%	40%	42%	24%	28%
Not worried	17%	24%	17%	45%	56%

Source: Newport People and Jobs Survey, 1981

Anxiety levels are also highest where other members of the household are unemployed and lowest where there are more in full-time work.

iv Health Effects - overall levels

We asked all of our main respondents, 307 people whether their health had been affected by the current jobs situation in Newport. If they said that it had, we asked them in what ways and what they had done about it.

First, how many people reported that their health had been affected by the jobs situation?

19% of the population in our sample reported adverse health effects. Table 47 shows the main people involved.

A very small number of those in other categories - retired, sick, students - reported any adverse health effects.

Table 46: Health effects of job situation		
	Health affected	Health not affected
All respondents	19%	81%

Source: Newport People and Jobs Survey, 1981

Table 47: Health effects of job situation: some main groupings		
Employment position	Health affected	Health not affected
In full-time work	17%	83%
In part-time work	19%	81%
Housewives	30%	70%
Unemployed	33%	67%

Source: Newport People and Jobs Survey 1981

Clearly, then, a higher proportion of those out of paid employment - full-time housewives and the unemployed - suffer ill health because of the local jobs situation than those in paid employment. Nonetheless, 17% of those in full-time work and 19% of those in part-time work also reported adverse health effects.

The effects are therefore general throughout the population, although they fall most heavily on full-time housewives and the unemployed.

v Changes in Employment and Health

Do changes in employment affect the picture? Change in employment status over a period of two years is not in itself the prime cause of health problems, but it does make matters worse. More people in stable positions over the whole period are ill (9.5% of the total population) and many more remain healthy (50% of the total population); this is because there are many more people in stable employment in the population anyway. But the proportion of those who become ill in the whole population rises with changes in employment status.

We asked people who said that their health had been affected if they would like to tell us more. Here are just some of their comments:

'I suffer from my nerves - its worry about the money.'

'I can't afford to eat so well.'

'Getting fatter and lazy. The wife has worried very badly.'

'Its affected my relationship with my husband - we bicker over money. Before he was redundant we didn't have to worry.'

'I'm a bag of nerves trying to stretch my money. Everything's going up - rent, coal, etc...'

'I had a heart attack - I think it's the strain of worrying from day to day that did it.'

'Had treatment for nerves - lost 2 to 3 stone in weight - when unemployed.'

'Nerve rashes. I get psoriasis when big bills come in.'

'Took an overdose.'

'I'm diabetic and stress is making me worse'.

'It makes me depressed. I always had good health before.'

'Worry has brought on bronchial trouble.'

'My husand has a lot of pressure at work - he's ill for the firsttime in years.'

'The strain has caused friction.'

'I've been off sick with worry, and my son too.'

'With the worry, I'm just not myself - it causes arguments in the family.'

'I worry about money - it affects my blood pressures.'

'You get uptight - I'm not so relaxed.'

'OK now. It was causing trouble at home, I was rowing with the wife.'

'The wife has felt the stress and strain'.

'Worry has affected my nerves, made me aggressive.'

'I'm not sleeping - the doctor's given me sleeping tablets.'

'When the baby was born 5 months ago I was so worried, it affected my nerves badly. I was getting really uptight.'

'I 've had a nervous breakdown... It's worse since I've been home with nothing to do. My wife keeps on at me to get a job, but the man at the Job Centre says there's none.'

'Last year I had a nervous breakdown worrying if I'd lose my job.'

'I've been a sick man for the last 12 months - prior to that I've never seen the doctor. I've a growth on my throat and stress doesn't help. I feel I've aged 10 years, through overwork.'

'I can't sleep sometimes...depressed...there's friction in the family.'

Table 48: Changes in Employment over 2 year period and health effects

No. of changes	Health affected	Health not affected
No change	16%	84%
One change	28%	72%
Two changes	50%	50%
Three changes	27%	73%
Four changes	25%	75%

Source: Newport People and Jobs Survey, 1981

Those who change most are in non-manual and unskilled groups, and least changes are recorded in managerial and professional groups. Nearly 64% of non-manual and 60% of unskilled workers in our sample changed their employment status at least once in the 2 year period. This represents respectively about 12% and 35.5% of the total working population in our sample.

And most change is concentrated in the younger age groups: 8.3% were aged under 20 years, 25% were between 20 and 34 years, 18.5% were between 35 and 49 years, and 12% were aged 50-64 years.

But it should be carefully noted that 23% of those currently in full-time jobs changed their employment status on one or more occasions in the last 2 years. This represents a larger number of people than for any groups other than the unemployed. We should therefore not assume that changes relate to unemployment alone. Many job changes cause anxiety which can lead to ill health.

vi Actual Health Effects

But how precisely is health affected? And are different people within the community affected differently? We asked people to describe the condition for themselves and their description fell into the categories in Table 49. People spoke in the main about mental ill health, serious enough in itself, but also the cause of many physical illnesses, as noted in the first part of this section of the report.

Table 49: Actual Health Effects	
Description of principal effect	Percentage of those reporting illnesses
Nervous conditions	33%
Depressive states	22.5%
Worry caused bad health	19%
Family strain and tension	19%
Existing ill health made worse	5%
Not sleeping	5%
Nervous breakdown	3.5%
Overdose/suicidal	3.5%

Source: Newport People and Jobs Survey, 1981

Are these health effects similar for all groups? First, let us compare those who have been unemployed with others.

Table 50: Health Effects: unemployed and employed				
	Unemployed at some point in the last 2 years		Employed throughout the last 2 years	
	% within category	% within total population	% within category	% within total population
Nervous conditions	39%	12%	61%	19%
Depressive state	54.5%	10.5%	45.5%	9%
Worry caused bad health	25%	3.5%	75%	10.5%
Family strain and tension	64%	12%	36%	7%
Existing ill health made worse	-	-	100%	3.5%
Not sleeping	50%	1.8%	50%	1.8%
Nervous breakdown	50%	1.8%	50%	1.8%
Overdose/suicidal	-	-	100%	3.5%

Source: Newport People and Jobs Survey, 1981

Let us look carefully at what this suggests. Because the unemployed are a smaller proportion of the total population, and health effects are spread through the community, those in employment will generally register higher numbers and percentages than any other particular group.

But there are significant differences:

- depressive states appear to affect the unemployed more markedly than the employed. Indeed, a DHSS official spoke of the emergence of the 'depressed unemployed', describing the large number of people experiencing 'more and more despair' because they really could not find jobs;

- family tensions were concentrated where there was unemployment;

- nervous conditions were heavily concentrated in those in full-time work, although the local secretary of MIND said that it had been the experience of his organisation that mental health problems increased as redundancy payments ran out. Indeed, it was a commonly held view that problems were to follow in large measure at this time in Newport;

- both full-time workers and the unemployed have their fair share of nervous breakdowns;

- housewives scored high in all categories.

However crude the distinctions, one can begin to see that although the root cause of people's problems may be similar - i.e. anxiety about the job situation - their precise circumstances are probably giving rise to quite different health conditions.

An interesting feature of this is that unemployed people and full-time housewives may have more in common than they think: they both have to create their own framework for daily life. Paid employment provides objectives, timetables, relationships, status and rewards. As Marie Jahoda says, paid employment satisfies the basic need a person has for a framework for daily life. Without this imposed framework, how can a person manage? And those out of work, or changing work most often, are also amongst the least able to cope. This presents, therefore, a major problem for people. It is a problem shared to some extent by housewives and the unemployed.

In our survey depression was heavily concentrated in the unemployed, and suicide attempts were exclusively concentrated in housewives.

We do not have sufficient data to comment on whether such abject distress as results in suicide is marginally more present in one part of the community than another. But it is clear that feelings of futility are not exclusively characteristic of unemployed people.

According to Brenner, suicide is 'virtually an economic indicator',[1] and suicides have increased since the mid-

---

1. Lecture given at the Heath Hospital, Cardiff, April 1979.

1970's. But others maintain that detailed analysis of the statistics does not suggest that unemployment and high suicide rates can be directly related'.[2] Furthermore, the Newport Samaritans, although they record increased enquiries, hear from a cross-section of the community about a whole range of problems.

Alcoholism is often mentioned as a consequence of unemployment. Brenner links alcoholism with economic stress, but he does not maintain that the unemployed will become alcoholic in greater numbers. Indeed, we can see that household expenditure on alcohol has decreased, and shops, pubs and clubs will confirm this.

Nevertheless, alcoholism is increasing and the gap between male and female alcoholics is narrowing.[3] However, the local branch of Alcoholics Anonymous say that their membership is broad and includes housewives and retired people.

I am therefore indicating the kind of analysis and discussion that could take place about the health consequences of the local jobs situation. I hope that I have made it clear that there is no simple analysis, many people are affected in many different ways. However, I have begun to draw distinctions as to how these differences are experienced, though more detailed work would be required to speak of them with confidence.

vii Health - seeking help

The health effects people experienced were serious enough for large numbers to seek help.

Table 51: Health effects: sources of help

Source of help	Overall percentage of those seeking help	Behaviour of particular groups: Full-time workers	Full-time Housewives	Unemployed
Doctor	52%	40%	71%	31%
Relative	34%	40%	14%	56%
Friend	3%	-	-	6%
Did not seek help	11%	20%	14%	6%

Source: Newport People and Jobs Survey, 1981

2. 'Suicide and Deliberate Self-Harm', Office of Health Economics, London, 1981
3. Social Trends, 1981, Central Statistical Office, HMSO

Table 51 shows the interesting phenomenon that relatively smaller proportions of the unemployed seek medical help resulting in fewer unemployed people seeing the doctor than other groups in the community who are ill. Considerably more seek the help of relatives and friends. Indeed, they represent the largest proportion of the total population who resolve their health problems in this way.

Full-time housewives top the list of those who see the doctor, and they form the largest proportion of the total population seeking medical help. But relatively few sought the help of relatives and, perhaps surprisingly, none said that they had sought help from friends. The General Household Survey[1] states that a higher proportion of women seek medical help, but it does not supply other comparative data.

The proportion of full-time workers who see the doctor follows some way behind housewives, but it still represents the second largest proportion of patients in the population. Large numbers also spoke to relatives about their illness. This must to some extent reflect the generally agreed view that fewer full-time workers are now spending time off work, even when ill, for fear they will lose their jobs.

This analysis should sound warning bells for those authorities which tend to analyse the extent of problems related to unemployment in terms of referrals to medical and social agencies. The problems exist whether or not they are currently resulting in noticeably increased referrals. And those who do seek help, although they are suffering from the effects of economic stress, are not necessarily unemployed. From the evidence in this report, one must question the adequacy of official statistics in defining and quantifying the extent of social and medical problems.

General Welfare

This survey has clearly established widespread anxiety in the community resulting in bad mental and physical health. Much of this can be put down to financial worries, again spread throughout the community. Pressure falls most heavily on the young, the unskilled, women and the unemployed, but it also falls on those in employment, and because this is still the largest group in the community, it often contains the highest incidence of ill health and other problems.

The social consequences of this do not appear to show through in referrals to local voluntary and statutory bodies.

---

1. General Household Survey, 1978, Office of Population Censuses and Surveys, HMSO.

A report produced by The Joint Working Party of Directors of Social Services and the Welsh Office (March 1980), based on Brenners approach, concerning unemployment and the Personal Social Services states that no significant increases in workloads have so far been reported, but that increases must be expected. Table 52 estimates the additional expenditure required to meet this projected demand.

Table 52: Unemployment and Social Service spending: Estimate of possible effect upon the need for some aspects of Personal Social Services spending following a 1% increase in the unemployment rate sustained for five years

	Estimated Expenditure in 1977-78 (£000s)	% increase needed	Estimated Additional Expenditure needed (Nov. 1980 figures £000s)
Residential for children in trouble	4,287	4.0%	172
Social work with children in trouble	2,376	4.0%	95
Social work with the mentally ill	513	3.4%	17
Other services for the mentally ill	576	3.4%	20
Social work with the sick and handicapped	2,196	1.9%	42
Other services for the sick and handicapped	3,854	1.9%	73
Administration, Training etc.	-	-	97
Total	-	-	516

Source: The Implications of Rising Unemployment for Personal Services in Wales. March 1980. Joint Working Party of Directors of Social Services in Wales and the Welsh Office.

It is greatly to be valued that assessments of this kind are taking place; I would only suggest that the additional problems exist already and that it is the delivery of services which now requires examination. For example, evidence from the survey points to the need for preventative and educative work now in the field of mental health. It is not appropriate to wait for the breakdown of some individuals before providing a service: such a supportive service would probably be helpful to very many and diverse people who will, hopefully, never reach the point of complete breakdown.

There is a certain degree of surprise in local organisations that welfare work-loads have not increased as a result of unemployment. Most also persist in the belief that they will do so eventually.

Our survey clearly shows that family tensions are concentrated in unemployed families, but this is not reflected in increased enquiries to relevant local organisations.

- The Catholic Marriage Advisory Council has had a 30% increase in work over the last 2 years, but relatively small numbers are involved and there is only slight evidence of a bias towards the unemployed.

- The same is true of the Gwent Marriage Guidance Council. Again, they report an increase in cases, but these are not seen in terms of unemployment: drink, sex, children and financial worries are the major problems.

- Newport Women's Aid confirmed this view. They are always busy and unemployment has not increased their work.

- A police spokesman believed that working wives may be staving off some family troubles and he too did not report any increase.

The Newport Citizen's Advice Bureau said that their enquiries had risen steadily over the years: from 913 in 1979 to 1,227 in 1980, for example, but that was really an indication of the growth of the CAB. The problems people brought? Consumer issues topped the list, followed by housing, family and personal problems. People came from all sectors of the community and there was no obvious link with increasing unemployment.

This same view was expressed by two other organisations with an overview of voluntary welfare: Gwent Volunteer Bureau and Gwent Community Services Council. But both did suggest that problems would eventually increase. This same general impression was frequently repeated.

Most of the social consequences I have examined are not those which can be solved by local organisations. They are essentially about people coping on low incomes and under stress. I was unable to examine the ways people are finding the support they need. Indeed, we know very little about the networks of help that exist among friends, neighbours and community organisations. Clearly social support is needed in order to improve health and well-being, and such support is not automatically available, especially on large and relatively modern housing estates. Extensive family links do not exist within those areas; and when work friends are no longer there, because of unemployment, a significant source of sustenance is removed. There is little doubt in my mind that much could be done to help people establish more fruitful networks of friends and neighbours through appropriate social and health care intervention within housing estates. That is in part the subject of the final section of this report - what sort of self-help is possible and practical in order to develop local economic and social enterprise?

CHAPTER THREE

DIRECTIONS FOR THE FUTURE

Attitudes Towards The Future

This chapter presents some ideas on options for action to help remedy the situation analysed in the foregoing sections. The ideas and judgements put forward here are those of the author alone and should not be taken as reflecting the views of any of the sponsoring bodies.

To put such possibilities in perspective, however, let us first glance at the attitudes (to their own future) of the people concerned.

Table 53. Jobs Situation - Attitudes Towards the Future

Attitude	% of respondents
Particularly concerned for young people	35%
Feeling hopeless/in despair	32%
Insecure about the future	20%
Angry about position	17%
Fear of violence from young people	8%
No hope: too old	6%
No hope: thinking of emigrating	3%
Secure about future	17%

Source: Newport People and Jobs Survey, 1981

And some of their comments:

'Defeated.'

'There's no hope - especially with my age. I'm a tradesman. I've applied for jobs all over the world. Even when the Job Centre has jobs for electricians abroad, or even here, they don't notify me. It's soul-destroying.'

'One son made redundant, it's hard. I'm working to make ends meet. What about my youngest - what chance has he?..'

'My future existence is non-existent. Every day in the Job Centre, there's nothing going, or only if you have qualifications.'

'We're stuck at our age - at 40 you're too old today. We're on the bread line.'

'We've been fortunate up to now, all working. I'm worried about my youngest daughter.'

'We're OK - just managing.'

'I'm going self-employed, confident it will be OK.'

'It's going to get worse. My firm has been taken over and there's a threat of redundancy. Three-quarters of the staff have already gone.'

'It doesn't affect me. I feel sorry for the youngsters.'

'I think I'll never work again because of my age. I've been made redundant three times. They tell me I'm too old.'

'It's grim. I've got to get a job, I've a daughter to support.'

'There is no future in Newport - there would have to be a dramatic change. We'll have to move out. But if we move, it might be like jumping out of the frying pan into the fire.'

'I can't see any future. There's nothing for the boys. They've just given up. They're moody and bored.'

'I don't think I'll ever get a job with all the young ones coming up.'

'We're worried sick. The only thing is you know everybody else is in the same boat. We worry most about the children.'

Regenerating Hope Through Local Action

During the study I was almost overwhelmed by the range and degree of personal distress arising from the local jobs situation. Sometimes I felt that nothing could be done that would help people on a sufficient scale. But positive measures are possible, and so long as they are imaginatively and boldly executed, they may well have considerable impact.

Furthermore, there is a recurring theme to help guide our actions. Throughout this report I have made references to the degree to which local autonomy exists. The local economy is controlled in large measure by government and business quite distant from the town. It is not simply a matter of control, but the town has become dependent on large employers and a relatively narrow base. Furthermore, people have come to rely on others to create work for them, and when this work is removed, the dependencies are laid bare. The personal and social consequences are considerable. The central question we must therefore address concerns the extent to which these dependencies can be reversed. What scope is there for locally generated economic and social solutions to our problems?

I will approach this in four parts:

* The need for a new focus and thrust to long-term strategic thinking and the promotion of local economic and social initiatives: some form of Town Economic and Social Development Group.

* The need to further stimulate and support local economic initiatives from the medium and small firm, to the co-operative or community enterprise.

* The need to create new social enterprises for those without employment.

* The need for study to promote continued developments on the basis of considered analysis.

I have separated the four areas for the sake of clarity, though in practice they would be interrelated.

A Town Social and Economic Development Group

Many local people feel defeated. They feel powerless to do anything about the position they are in. They have become dependent on others for solutions. In this instance, they look to Government.

We asked what people thought could be done to improve the jobs situation in the town. We did not prompt them other than to ask, where appropriate, if they felt anything could be done locally. Table 54 shows the results.

The scale of the social consequences of unemployment - the essential subject of this report - leaves talk of solutions unconvincing. Instead we should concentrate energies where positive results are possible. The basic direction of social policy should be towards self-help in developing the local economy. It is at this point that human and economic needs overlap: the two aspects of local life are interlinked.

But it should not be thought that a new focus on the development of the local economy will result in dramatic numbers of new jobs: like all major changes it will prove to be complex, difficult and long-term.

Table 54. Jobs Situation: What can be done?[1]	
Action	% of Respondents
Nothing locally	31%
Change the Government	30%
Improve opportunities for young people	21.5%
Increase council public works	6%
Introduce earlier retirement	6%
Lower wages	5%
Increase business incentives	5%

Source: Newport People and Jobs Survey - 1981

A number of organizations have been hard at work in recent years to attract new industry to Newport, and to help existing firms in the town.[2] A fresh initiative based on regeneration within the community itself should be seen as complementary to those efforts rather than being in competition with them.

Whatever success we can reasonably expect from all these efforts to create jobs, unemployment is likely to continue to rise for some time and is likely to remain high thereafter. Therefore, as much energy and imaginative new thinking needs to go into finding satisfying alternative social enterprises for those without employment. Such enterprises should not only avoid the worst consequences of unemployment, but provide dignified and necessary work for as many people as possible.

---

1. Small numbers thought that: the Government was doing its best; wages were too low; national service should be reintroduced; jobs were available; we should leave the EEC; improve the careers service; provide more leisure; stop supplementary benefits; and stop immigration.

2. These organizations include Newport Borough Council, Welsh Office, Department of Industry, Welsh Development Agency and BSC (Industries) Ltd.

We are therefore talking about the regeneration of a town if we are to replace despair with hope. The task is enormous. A new and significant initiative is needed which will command attention and which will publicly promote this regeneration. Some way of providing this focus therefore needs to be sought out. Perhaps a new single group should be established: let us call it the Newport Economic and Social Development Group. This should consist of all those most powerfully concerned with local economic and social life: industry, trade unions, local government, government agencies and local organisations and individuals. But if it is to be dynamic the group should remain small. Furthermore, it would need specific responsibilities confirmed by the Council and important local bodies.

The group should not be narrowly based, but capable of:

* creating and promoting a long-term strategy for local economic and social initiatives involving the widest section of the community;

* promoting new ideas within the framework of that strategy.

This group would not be easy to set up, but the benefits could be considerable. If it is to work it would need to contain people selected because they could do the job: it would need to be small; it would need to be free from bureaucratic obstacles; it would need to be given responsibility and status; and it would need to be adequately serviced, possibly through a secondment from local industry or the local authority.

Secondments from industry and commerce could be arranged through Action Resource in Wales, an organisation specifically set up to arrange secondments to community enterprises.

If such a body were established, it could greatly facilitate co-ordinated action and could review new ideas speedily. There are plenty of ideas, the problem is to examine them efficiently and, if appropriate, to implement them. Some are well developed elsewhere: Working Communities, pioneered by a group of London architects and taken up by BSC (Industries) Ltd., are a way in which a large number of small independent companies can share premises and facilities so enjoying services normally only available in large companies. There is a manager who is able to advise the companies in their development. BSC (Industries) Ltd. is intent on developing such a project in Newport, but there is probably scope for a variety of working communities in and around the town.

Elsewhere, local authorities are setting up Municipal Enterprises, which examine the Council's purchasing policies and encourage local production wherever possible.

I mention these ideas to point out the current difficulty of doing appropriate research and feasibility work relatively quickly and efficiently in order to capitalise on ideas that would help the town: the appropriate organisation does not exist.

Promoting Local Economic Initiative

If the Town Economic and Social Development Group is essential for strategic thinking and the formation of fresh initiatives, there should also be action units either established by it or closely related to it. What is probably required is:

* a Local Business Promotions Unit
* a Co-operative and Community Enterprise Unit

I will deal with each in turn.

i Local Business Promotions Unit

The experience of the St. Helen's Trust in Merseyside is helpful here. This is a Local Enterprise Trust, an independent company set up by all the major local bodies involved in industrial life: local authorities, banks, unions, industry, and commerce. Antony Pilkington is the chairman.

The trust exists to help any new business in the town and claims to have helped to create 500 new jobs and to have sustained 500 others in its first two years.

A good record by any standards and at a modest cost: four of the five staff are seconded either from the banks or Pilkingtons, leaving only the cost of the organiser.

The essence of the local enterprise trust is that it can act as a kind of switchboard, helping new businesses to plug into the huge local resources that are already available in the major firms and institutions. But St. Helens, in particular, also works alongside new business through all the formative stages and then as appropriate afterwards.

There is no doubt that this simple mechanism works. It also works in the Hackney Business Promotions Centre.

Again at a modest cost of £20,000 major initiatives have been undertaken.

A Business Promotions Unit established in Newport could give the focus that is needed for a new long-term effort to develop the local medium and small firm, and it would be charged with encouraging new local enterprise in every way possible. It would be visible, approachable and flexible and, most importantly, it would be able to call upon the resources already in the community, in business, the professions and local government.

A Business Promotions Unit is exclusively concerned with conventional commercial enterprise. The community or voluntary organisation has no positive role to play here.

ii Co-operatives and Community Enterprises

Springing up around the country there are new kinds of businesses, sometimes in the form of a community enterprise and sometimes as a co-operative.

'A community enterprise is usually a trading organisation, owned and controlled by the residents of a given area and set up to create permanent jobs for local people in viable enterprises. Such a community company will recycle profits either into the development of new enterprises (and thus additional jobs) or into benefitting the local community in some other way.'[1]

These enterprises are most highly developed in Scotland. I spent a week touring them with another member of the steering group for this project. We saw a wide range of initiatives, including:

- Goodwill Incorporated: which collects and recycles furniture and other household items and sells them through its own shop in Glasgow.

- Govan Enterprises: an umbrella company for a number of small scale efforts: a grain store, badge making, and a market.

- Craigmillar Enterprises: a building company employing 12 workers.

- Port Glasgow Community Enterprises: their first initiative is a scheme for craft outworkers and a shop called Pegleg.

---

1. John Pearce and Pat Cassidy, Can We Make Jobs? BBC Publications, June 1980.

These enterprises are supported by staff from the Scottish Council of Social Services and the specialist, Local Enterprises Advisory Project, based in Paisley - this has four fieldworkers and a small consultancy fund for feasibility work.

I did a detailed analysis of co-operatives based upon the 1980 directory[2]. The following figures are approximate because it is not possible to be precise from the information provided:

- well over 60% of jobs in co-operatives are concentrated in the top 27 co-ops;

- most co-ops are based on printing, wholefoods and books: not work for unskilled people;

- 83 out of a total of 330, just over 25%, were based in Greater London.

For co-operatives to make an impact in a town like Newport, they would need to be more broadly based and numerous. Everywhere where co-operative development is being seriously considered some fundamental change is being sought to give real backing to their growth: usually some form of bank or special funding.

The type of co-operative developed by the Highlands and Islands Development Board (HIDB) has relevance to a town like Newport. The community co-operative is one in which large numbers of the local community have shares. It is democratically run but functions as a viable enterprise. The community co-operative can then establish a variety of small co-operatives: it is therefore a multi-function co-operative.

The HIDB helps by providing fieldwork support in the first instance to bring the co-ops into existence, and thereafter through continuing back-up service. Grants matching local subscriptions are put in, the salary of a manager for up to 5 years is provided, and further finance is considered under the normal HIDB grants and loans schemes. This form of organisation provides the kind of substantial backing required by co-operatives and community enterprises alike.

Community enterprises and co-operatives have defects which can be put right:

- inadequate funding: little is needed, but the right amount is essential for positive growth;

- paternalistic funding in the form of grants which demand little of the initiators is destructive; if they are necessary at all, matching grants are appropriate;

---

2. Co-ops: A Directory of Industrial and Service Co-operatives. Autumn 1980. Co-operative Development Agency.

- confusion about the purpose of the organisation: is it there for social or commercial purposes? It can be both, but we should only be interested in viable enterprise;

- inadequate feasibility work simply stores up problems.

But some problems are more fundamental:

- successful business people are unlikely to become involved and so the co-operative or community enterprise is likely always to suffer through lack of experience and aptitude for business;

- community groups generally lack the necessary discipline and flexibility for business and it is difficult to know how or even if this can be overcome, but if the group involved is determined enough, this is half the battle: good feasibility work and open, experienced consultancy support would also greatly help.

Community enterprises and co-operatives should be encouraged. The contribution will be modest but positive. A unit based upon the HIDB model would be appropriate for Newport. Two or three fieldworkers, one or two possibly seconded from business, would be adequate in the first place, and a small back-up fund would be essential.

The Community Projects Foundation has submitted a detailed proposal to the Council to establish a unit to develop community-based economic employment initiatives.

New Social Enterprise

The social consequences of economic stress are deep and widespread: that at least can be gleaned from this report. But the onerous burdens on the most vulnerable - the young, families with children, women and the unemployed - need to be lifted.

The consequences most often emanate from financial hardship which causes stress, then ill health, and sometimes crime and other social problems. The only way to effectively solve these problems is to create sufficient jobs, but we know that this will not be possible. We are also now aware that technological developments will render high levels of unemployment a permanent feature of our society, at least for the foreseeable future.

There is therefore a twofold need: firstly, to relieve the residual distress caused by hardship and to strengthen people's capacities to survive, and secondly, to create new forms of social enterprises that will provide creative work, on products or services which are needed by society.

Here we run into too many intangibles. But one can point to practical possibilities arising from the report:

- health education concerning stress and how to cope with it; counselling and training services by people already at work in housing estates and factories; unemployed people could also be trained as health workers in this field;

- financial information is needed: what is the extent of under-claiming in benefits and how can this be remedied? Could new forms of credit union be established in the town?

- what action can be taken for the long-term unemployed? In particular, what is the scope for workshops which make socially useful products? Could these be integrated with well-established enterprises so that movement into full-time work is possible?

- are there areas of the town where in-depth work can be mounted in order to strengthen existing sources of help and especially the networks between neighbours, friends and organisations which provide mutual support?

How can we take further these and similar ideas? This report could be given wide circulation among local voluntary and statutory bodies to elicit their views on it and to encourage them to engage in the practical developments emerging at this time.

South Gwent Community Aid has decided to try to co-ordinate the efforts of local organisations in this field and their efforts might be given support by the Council.

Economic and Social Analysis

Many people instinctively reject research. In our present conditions this is folly. Part of the problem about doing good research is to get the results examined and acted upon. Research, in other words, demands flexibility and invites a response on the part of others. One-off pieces of work are of limited value. A long-term intelligence, feasibility and study function could be an important component in the local build up of knowledge and action.

A good deal of basic data is being generated by public bodies, but no in-depth research is being done about the Newport economy. It is badly needed. This research is far too general: it barely scratches the surface. We should know a great deal more, especially for planning and forecasting purposes. Studies of the employment patterns of different working groups, the needs of small businesses, the employment conditions of young people - these are some of the relevant and important subjects for study.

It is important to monitor the social consequences of unemployment: to study the effects on particular groups: in particular the young, housewives and the elderly, so as to build policies and services on that knowledge. Too often the problems have to fit policies and established practices rather than the other way around.

At present the priority in Newport as far as the public is concerned is to do something positive about the position of young people: the under 20s. This would have universal support for there is a deep concern either about or for young people within all sections of the community. More people spoke with feeling on this subject than any other.

Some of them spoke of their criticisms of government schemes, especially WEEP (Work Experience on Employer's Premises). Here are some of the things they said:

> 'WEEP is an easy thing for employers - instead of paying £60 properly, they get away with £23 from the Government. My parents and grandparents fought against this sort of thing - child labour.'

> 'Why is all the money spent on WEEP not spent on proper jobs? The youngsters are expected to work a full week for a third of the money others are getting.'

> 'Government schemes - I worked in one, but they take advantage of you. It's cheap labour.'

> 'Government youth schemes are putting older people out of work. This government is blind, it doesn't think.'

> 'Before I was made redundant they took on 6 WEEP boys - then they sacked 4 of us....the boys are doing the same job as me.'

> 'My daughter is on WEEP - it's a racket. They should be making them full-time jobs - employers take advantage.'

A jobs vacuum has been created for young people, and government schemes do not adequately fill it. Too much of the stress, uncertainty and sheer lack of hope is concentrated on young shoulders: time after time in earlier sections of this report we discovered that the incidence of unemployment, redundancy, stress or ill health fell disproportionately on the under 20s.

A review of the position of young people could provide a comprehensive plan for an integrated scheme of information, training and community enterprises that would win the approval of young people and relevant government agencies. The views of young people should be canvassed as fully as possible. A small group from the Council could monitor the review and the advice of the National Youth Bureau, an organisation respected for its knowledge on this subject, might well be sought as to how the review could best be undertaken.

WAYS AHEAD: AN AFTERWORD

Community Projects Foundation

The purpose of the present research was to find out and describe the effects of unemployment in Newport. This has led the researcher, in concluding, to suggest some avenues for remedial action.

The picture of possible ways forward can be substantially amplified by indicating some of the kinds of action which are already (in February 1982) at an advanced stage of consideration by Newport Borough Council. The genesis of this report lies, indeed, in the Council's concern to alleviate the problems described.

The Borough Council's Initiative

The producers of this report, Community Projects Foundation, cannot, of course, speak for the Council or represent its overall intentions. CPF has, however, been participating, at the Council's request, in intensive discussions aimed at producing a plan for remedial action. It will give some indication of the scope of those plans to include here a brief account of the CPF contribution.

It must be stressed that what follows is not to be taken as a description of the whole of the Council's plan as such. In any case, such plans are of course subject to further decisions of the Council at every stage.

The account below is confined to the <u>principles</u> of the CPF contribution, since the specifics may undergo further modification as action proceeds. In adding these concluding remarks to the report, CPF development staff are affirming a belief that the principles, which have been culled from experience among their own projects and reported by some others who have been active in this field will stand for some time to come as a useful approach to problems of unemployment in a given locality. As regards their specific application in Newport they can, of course, only be regarded as accurate in February 1982.

The Council's overall plan is centred on the establishment of an enterprise trust consisting of representatives from BSC (Industries) Ltd, Newport Borough Council itself, the Community Projects Foundation and possibly a number of other bodies.

The trust would foster schemes to create new economic activity in Newport. It would appoint a director and finance adviser, maintain a workshop, and establish a unit with the task of creating development programmes. The CPF contribution is concerned primarily with the functions of the development unit, and is based on the following reasoning.

Economic Predicament and Social Crisis

Communities which face large scale redundancies, particularly where employment is concentrated in one sector of industry, undergo a process in which the effects on the individual are progressively intensified. The erosion of social networks, patterns of relationships and indigenous institutions follows from economic decline. Policy responses which seek only to expand existing styles of service and delivery are not adequate. What is needed, as well as economic assistance, is the rebuilding of community life.

CPF's current work on employment-related issues frequently makes use of two parallel concepts originating in other fields - crisis intervention and community economics:

Crisis intervention is a concept borrowed from social casework. According to the International Encyclopedia of the Social Sciences (London: Collier Macmillan, 1972) social theorists maintain that the vulnerability of the individual during a crisis produced by changes in life-situation can, in certain conditions, prove to be fertile ground for long-term improvement. Individuals differ in their capacity to mobilise their latent potential, and the quality of social support available to the person can considerably influence the outcome. It is important that professional helpers should be ready to intervene in favour of solutions which will increase self-confidence, maturity and ability to cope with stress. The aim is to prevent a downward spiral of morale, or the consolidation of rigid and brittle defences. These concepts of individual behaviour and need would seem to be equally applicable to communities.

Community economics simply means the analysis of activity within a community, be it a neighbourhood, town or region, in economic terms. Within the boundaries of a given area, imports and exports can be indentified, balance of payments accounts can be constructed, and similar exercises can be undertaken for investment levels, as is done for national economies. It is not assumed that the local economy is self-sufficient: the exercise allows one to see how the 'mini-economy' is dependent on forces and decisions arising outside its boundaries. Community economics highlights the lack of control exercised locally in economically-depressed areas.

The basis of community-work experience is in the social rather than economic area, and it is the ultimate effect on community life which remains our principle concern. The present note, however, is confined to presenting an economic strategy for local development - a strategy which concentrates on the fostering of new small-scale economic enterprises. Broadly, then, the ideas are about 'small business' - where the term is understood to cover a whole range of possible enterprises: not only traditional private enterprise but co-operatives, shared-workshop schemes, 'umbrella' companies providing centralised services to otherwise isolated self-employed people, and whatever viable new forms of enterprise can be devised.

A primary aim of community work is to identify the strengths of a community and reinforce them before they lose their vitality. Small successes can alter the sense of an inexorable downward spiral of failure. It is essential to encourage autonomous learning and activity amongst people who in the past may have seen little reason to believe that such effort could benefit them. Any improvement in local economies will depend, for its lasting effect, on the extent to which it is complemented by an improvement in people's ability to organise themselves to satisfy their needs and enhance the prospects for their community. The aim of providing the kinds of help detailed below is therefore not merely the provision of a service but, so far as possible, the gradual transfer of the specified skills to the people who need to draw on them.

The Role of Small Business in Economic Regeneration

The difficult economic climate of recent years has prompted a number of individuals and organisations to propose ways in which the economic life of an area can be improved by small-scale local action. Key features of local economic life which need to be analysed for this purpose would include imports to the locality which could be substituted by domestic production, and activities which use the area only as a resource (either for output or consumption), and which could be made to contribute more to the locality.

CPF's interest in small businesses has developed from its community and youth work. Community-work is based on expertise in fostering personal development through the development of groups and organisations. The skills involved include recruitment, practical education, use of experts, organising work-experience, counselling, and running training workshops. These skills are relevant to business activity as well as to community-work.

'Small business' is usually defined in terms of numbers of employees and financial turnover. A more qualitative description has been put forward by the International Labour Organisation in Small Enterprise Development: Policies and Programmes (London: ILO,1977). Small businesses are those in which policy-making, management and execution are closely allied - often carried out by the same people; in which the operation is usually carried out in close proximity to its markets; in which risks taken, personalities involved and technology employed all have rapid effects; and in which there is not usually much readily-available finance.

Community-work's natural interest in small business development prompts a restatement of the potential of these kinds of enterprise for contributing to the reinvigoration of depressed communities. The main points identified by the ILO are:

- future economic development requires viable small as well as large enterprises;

- large enterprises need viable small enterprises to serve their needs;

- small enterprises can be economically efficient and effective;

- small enterprises can be a major source of innovation and entrepreneurial activity;

- small businesses have a propensity for labour-intensity and job creation at a relatively low capital level;

- most areas have people with small-enterprise managerial interest and talent;

- small firms have an important role to play in social development, particularly in providing stability and viability to communities in declining areas.

The range of assistance available to small businesses from government and other agencies is expanding. Most activity in this area is spontaneous and unco-ordinated. Until recently the major mode of intervention was advisory (for example, the nationwide Small Firms Advisory Service). This kind of help is reactive in character: the service is dependent on the client's initiative in asking for help. There is little active involvement in the development of business ideas or resolving problems in client firms.

Experience in social development programmes shows the limitations of an essentially passive approach, particularly in disadvantaged areas. This is not to suggest that such services do not meet a number of needs. But a more radical approach, which could be termed 'pro-active', needs to be developed, as it has been in the social field.

Present approaches to local economic regeneration are often fragmented. Most of the services concentrate on one area. For example, start-up finance is seldom tied to, or provided by, organisations providing technical or managerial assistance.

The effects of such a lack of co-ordination can be seen in the proliferation of organisations proffering advice to the small firm. Whilst this increases the businessman's ability to shop around for the most appropriate advice, it also engenders, for the assisting agencies, problems of reponsibility and authority.

The failure of small business associations and local employers' associations to enter the small-firm development arena is symptomatic of the general fragmentation.

There are, however, some examples of more co-ordinated approaches in this country. Best-established of these are the activities of the investment trusts, who often link their equity stakes to the appointment of a managing director or board member. Some trusts have been investing increasingly in smaller firms.

The ideas developed by the International Labour Organisation offer a useful framework for the kinds of assistance which a community-based programme might hope to contribute towards the development of local enterprise. Three main types of help are envisaged - developmental, managerial and technical.

Development assistance might include such things as conducting pre-investment studies, identifying prospective owners, preparing project proposals, providing some initial finance, advice on accounting, and investigating sub-contracting, franchising and licensing possibilities.

Managerial assistance might include management and worker training, establishment of organisational structure, advice on recruitment and selection, legal and financial advice, sales and distribution advice, and suggestions on how to manage production.

Technical assistance might include advice on materials and machinery, production techniques, working conditions, common service facilities, industrial research facilities, and design.

The ILO suggest that it is at the pre-project stage that the small business-person is usually most receptive to outside assistance, prepared to invest time, money and effort in attending development programmes, which is not likely to happen at all easily once the day-to-day pressures of maintaining the enterprise are encountered. But the firm's later development will also need outside support, and this may be best managed by forming links between small firms. The effectiveness of resource institutions may be increased when directed towards groups, and such groups also have potential for the sharing of experience.

The precise applicability of these ideas to Newport will be worked out in practice over a period of time. Certainly no claim is made that the development of small community enterprises can, on its own, solve the immense economic and social problems of our time. What the Development Unit idea does offer is a stimulus at the 'micro' level which should have the effect of demonstrating that the individual and the community need not remain helpless in the face of economic decline if they are willing to develop new approaches to the task of sustaining life.

Selected Reading

Selected Reading

The following is a selection of useful literature.

P.D. Anthony (1978) The Ideology of Work London: Tavistock

T. Austrin and H. Beynon (undated) Global Outpost. The Working Class Experience of Big Business in the North East of England 1964-1979 Department of Sociology, University of Durham, Elvet Riverside, Durham

D. Bell (1973) The Coming of the Post-Industrial Society Harmondsworth: Penguin

D.L. Birch (1979) The Job Generation Process Massachusetts Institute of Technology, Cambridge, Mass. USA.

H. Braverman (1974) Labour and Monopoly Capital New York: Monthly Review Press

M.H. Brenner (1973) Mental Illness and the Economy Harvard University Press

M.H. Brenner (1976) Estimating the Social Costs of National Economic Policy: Implications for Mental and Physical Health and Criminal Aggression Joint Economic Committee. Congress of the United States, Paper No.5. US Government Printing Office, Washington DC.

M.H. Brenner (1979) 'Mortality and the National Economy: A Review and the Experience of England and Wales 1936-1976.' The Lancet, September 15th.

British Association for the Advancement of Science (1978) Technology Choice and the Future of Work London: BAAS

CDP Political Economy Collective (1977) The Aims of Industry? A Study of Industrial Decline in the Community CDPPEC: Brookside, Seaton Burn, Newcastle upon Tyne

CDP Political Economy Collective (1979) The State and the Local Economy (Available as above)

M. College (1981) Unemployment and Health North Tyneside Community Health Council

W.W. Daniel (1972) Whatever Happened to the Workers in Woolwich? A Survey of Redundancy in SE London London: Political and Economic Planning

W.W. Daniel (1974) A National Survey of the Unemployed London: Political and Economic Planning

P. Eisenberg and P.F. Lazarfeld (1938) The Psychological Effects of Unemployment Psychological Bulletin 35

C. Evans (1979) The Mighty Micro London: Victor Gollancz

L. Fagin (1981) Unemployment and Health in Families DHSS

N. Falk et al (1980) Local Economic Development: A Guide to US Experience Urbed Research Trust, 359 The Strand, WC2

B. Ford (Ed) 'The Culture of Unemployment' New Universities Quarterly Vol.34 No. 1 Winter 1979/80 Oxford: Blackwell

S. Fothergill and G. Gudgin (1979) The Job Generation Process in Britain London: Centre for Enviromental Studies

J.I. Gershuny and R.E. Pahl (1980) 'Britain in the Decade of the three Economies' New Society 3rd January

B.H. Gottlieb, Ed. (1981) Social Networks and Social Support London: Sage

R.H. Gurrey (1980) 'The Effects of Unemployment on the Psycho-Social Development of School-Leavers.' Journal of Occupational Psychology 53

R. Harrison (1976) 'The Demoralising Experience of Prolonged Unemployment' Department of Employment Gazette April

K. Hawkins (1979) Unemployment Pelican Original. Harmondswoth: Penguin

J. Hayes and P. Nutman (1981) Understanding the Unemployed London: Tavistock Publications

W. Hannington (1973) Unemployed Struggles 1919-1936 Wakefield: EP Publishing Ltd.

W. Hannington (1976) The Problems of the Distressed Areas Wakefield: EP Publishing Ltd.

J.M.M. Hill (1978) 'The Psychological Impact of Unemployment' New Society 19th January

M.J. Hill, R.M. Harrison, A.V. Sargeant and V. Talbot (1973) Men Out of Work Cambridge University Press

G. Humphrys (1972) Industrial South Wales Newton Abbot: David and Charles

M. Jahoda, P. Lazarfeld, H. Zeigal (1933/72) Marienthal: The Sociography of an Unemployed Community London: Tavistock Publications

M. Jahoda and H. Rush (1980) Work, Employment and Unemployment Science Policy Research Unit, University of Sussex

C. Jenkins and B. Sherman (1979) The Collapse of Work London: Eyre Methuen

M. Jones (1972) Life on the Dole London: Davis-Poynter

H.R. Kahn (1964) The Repercussions of Redundancy London: Allen and Unwin

S.V. Kasl, S. Cobb, S. Gore (1972) 'Changes in Reported Illness and Illness Behaviour Related to Termination of Employment: A Preliminary Report' International Journal of Epidemeology Volume 2, Oxford University Press

R. Lister and F. Field (1978) Wasted Labour Child Poverty Action Group

M. Mann (1973) Workers on the Move Cambridge University Press

Manpower Services Commission (1981) Youth Unemployment and Special Measures: An Annotated Bibliography MSC

D. Marsden and E. Duff (1981 2nd Edition) Workless: Some Unemployed Men and their Families London: Croom Helm

T. McKeown (1976) The Modern Rise of Population London: Edward Arnold

S. Mukherjee (1973) Through No Fault of Their Own London: MacDonald for PEP

Newcastle Policy Services Department (1980) The Conseqences of the Closure of Vickers Elswick Defence Division Newcastle City Council

Newcastle Policy Services Department (1980) Redundancy in Newcastle Upon Tyne: A Case Study Newcastle City Council

R. Newnham (1980) Community Enterprise: British Potential and American Experience Department of Geography, Reading University

C. Pond (Ed) (1981) Low Pay Review March. Low Pay Unit

G. Rees and T.L. Rees (Eds) (1980) Poverty and Social Inequality in Wales London: Croom Helm

R. Rowthorn and T. Ward. 'How to run a company and run down an economy: the effects of closing down steel making in Corby.' Cambridge Journal of Economics 3, 1979

E.F. Schumacher (1979) Good Work London: Cape

B. Showler and A. Sinfield, (Eds) (1981) The Workless State Oxford: Martin Robertson

A. Sinfield (1981) What Unemployment Means Oxford: Martin Robertson

J. Thornley (1981) Workers' Cooperatives: Jobs and Dreams London: Heinemann Educational

P. Townsend (1979) Poverty in the United Kingdom Allen Lane

B. Ward (1979) Progress for a Small Planet Harmondsworth: Penguin

D. Weir, Ed. (1973) Men and Work in Modern Britain London: Fontana

D. Wedderburn (1964) White Collar Redundancy Cambridge: Cambridge University Press

D. Wedderburn (1965) Redundancy and the Railwaymen Cambridge: Cambridge University Press

R. Williams (1976) Keywords Glasgow: Fontana

P. Willis (1978) Learning to Labour: How Working Class Kids Get Working Class Jobs Farnborough: Saxon House

Appendix One

Survey Characteristics

PEOPLE AND JOBS IN NEWPORT - SURVEY CHARACTERISTICS

The survey 'People and Jobs' was carried out on Bettws and Ringland. A random sample of households was taken from the electoral register. Two pilot studies were conducted and the final survey completed between July 7th - 21st 1981. The results were analysed by the Sociological Research Unit at University College, Cardiff, using the Standard Package for the Social Sciences programme.

The following table is a breakdown of the number of interviews attempted and the rate of success we achieved.

Table 55: Survey characteristics

	Bettws	Ringland	Overall
	No.	No.	No.
Total households	3,007	2,444	5,451
Households: Total attempted	199	168	367
Houses unoccupied	1	-	1
Total included in sample	198	168	366
This represents about 1:15 of households, with 56% of interviews in Bettws and 44% in Ringland.			
Of these: No replies	8	17	25
Refusals	18	16	34
	26	33	59
Completed Questionnaires	172	135	307
Overall response rate:	87%	80%	84%

The table on the next page is a breakdown of the basic characteristics of the survey population.

Table 56: Survey: Population Characteristics

Characteristics	Number	Percentage
Main respondent:		
Males	109	35.5%
Females	198	64.5%
	307	100.0%
Total Sample:		
Males	338	48.0%
Females	363	52.0%
	701	100.0%
Households:		
Adult living alone	43	14.0%
Adults in household - no children	108	35.0%
Adults in household - with children	143	47.0%
Single parent household	13	4.0%
	307	100.0%

Single parent households represented just over 8% of households with children, a little below the average of about 10%.

		Households		Total People	
		No.	%	No.	%
Where children:					
Number of children:	1	66	42%	66	22%
	2	54	34%	104	35%
	3	27	17%	81	28%
	4	2	2%	8	3%
	5	7	5%	35%	12%
		156	100%	294	100%
Where adults:					
Number of adults:	2	166	66%	332	52%
	3	44	18%	132	20%
	4	30	12%	120	19%
	5	8	3%	40	6%
	6	3	1%	18	3%
		251	100%	642	100%

Ages	Number	Percentage
16-19	98	14.0%
20-34	199	28.0%
35-49	218	31.0%
50-64	132	19.0%
65+	49	7.0%
unknown	5	1.0%
	701	100.0%

Appendix Two

Survey Questionnaire

The questionnaire is a complex one and not easy to follow. As you read it you should imagine that respondents would be moving through the survey in a variety of patterns depending upon their particular circumstances.

Although the questionnaire was piloted on two occasions and we were highly satisfied with it for most purposes, questions 21 and 33 h are inadequate in determining socio-economic groupings.

PEOPLE AND JOBS IN NEWPORT - SURVEY QUESTIONNAIRE

(INTERVIEWER - Cover the following points - partly in your own words)

1. I am from a study group in Newport - South Gwent Community Aid - which is looking at ways to improve local employment, and services for the unemployed.

2. The group contains representatives from local organisations, Newport Council and voluntary bodies - and is serviced by a researcher.

3. They will be putting a report to Newport Council and others to recommend what can be done locally.

4. To make sure that the right things are done, we need to learn more about how the jobs situation in Newport is affecting people - and what their views are.

5. We are hoping to interview as many people as we can, like this at the door.

6. Everything will be treated in strict confidence, but we will keep a list of addresses until August so that the general results of the study can be posted through your door - just to let those who help us know about what we learn.

7. Could I therefore ask you some questions - it will only take about 15 minutes.

ADDRESS: ______________________ Identifier ☐

______________________ ☐

______________________ ☐

____

Card Number 1

1. Bettws 2. Ringland Area Code ☐

CALL LOG:

		Time	Date	Code
1. House unoccupied	Call 1	____	____	☐
2. Away/holidays				
3. No reply	Call 2	____	____	☐
4. No adults in the house				
5. Refused	Call 3	____	____	☐

INTERVIEWER: ______________________

I want to ask you later on for some information about any other adults in the household, but I would first of all like to ask you some questions about your own employment situation.

1. Do you currently have: (ring more than one if necessary)

   1. A full-time job)
   2. A part-time job) if only 2 or 3 ringed go
   3. A casual job) to Q.3
   4. None of these go to Q.5

2. Have you been on short-time working at any time in the last 4 weeks?

   1. Yes 2. No 8. DK 9. NA

3. Could you please tell me approximately how many hours per week you have worked in the last 4 weeks?

   1. Under 10 5. 35-39
   2. 10-19 6. 40-44
   3. 20-29 7. 45+
   4. 30-34

   Last week ☐

   Week before last ☐

   3 weeks ago ☐

   4 weeks ago ☐

4. Thinking about your current job, would you say that it is a secure job? (Probe for precise coding)

   1. Very secure 5. Very insecure
   2. Fairly secure 8. DK
   3. Secure 9. NA
   4. Insecure

5. Are you seeking employment at the moment?

   1. Yes 2. No

   If YES go to Q.7

6. If you are not seeking work at the moment, is there any particular reason? (Ring only one please)

   1. The work I have is satisfactory Go to Q.12
   2. Retired Go to Q.19
   3. Full-time housewife Go to Q.9
   4. Student/training Go to Q.12
   5. Sick/Ill Go to Q.12
   6. Other reason ________________ Go to Q.11
   8. DK 9. NA

7. How many jobs would you say that you have applied for since you have been looking for work?

1. Applied for none	4. 11-15	8. DK
2. 1-15	5. 16-20	9. NA
3. 6-10	6. 21+	

8. How long do you think it will be before you get a job?

1. Within a month
2. Within 3 months
3. Within 6 months
4. Within a year
5. When the economy picks up
6. Never have another job
7. Other (write in) ______________________
8. DK
9. NA

Go to Q.11

9. If the opportunity arose and you were offered a job, would you take it?

1. Yes   2. No   8. DK

10. Why is that do you think? ______________________

____

____

If No to Q.9 go to Q.12

11. (a) Are you currently registered as looking for work?

1. Yes   2. No   8. DK

If YES or DK to (a)

(b) Are you registered with any of the following:

1. Job Centre	3. PER
2. Careers Office	8. DK

12. Now I would like to get an accurate record of your employment position over the last two years.

Starting with your current position:

(a) You are? (read out categories and code as many as appropriate in column on right)

1. Full time employment
2. Part-time employment
3. In casual employment
4. Retired
5. Housewife
6. Unemployed (not in work but actively seeking a job)
7. Student/training
8. Sick/Ill
9. Other ________________
A. DK

	Employment position Code1	Code2	Code3	Time (weeks)
Current				
Column	36	37	38	39
Before that				
Column	40	41	42	43
Before that				
Column	44	45	46	47
Before that				
Column	48	49	50	51
Before that				
Column	52	53	54	55

(b) How long have you been in that position (answer in weeks in the extreme right-hand column)

INTERVIEWER: Repeat for all previous periods until the 2 year period is covered.

INTERVIEWER: THE FOLLOWING 4 QUESTIONS NEED TO BE ASKED IN ADDITION TO THE INFORMATION IN Q.12

- -

Let me just check:

13. Have you been unemployed at any time in the last 2 years?

1. Yes 2. No 8.DK

If NO go to Q.17

14. How many times have you been unemployed during the last 2 years?

1 2 3 4 5 6 7+ 8.DK

15. What was the longest period of unemployment in the last 2 years? (weeks) ☐

16. What was the shortest period of unemployment in the last 2 years? ☐

17. Have you been made redundant from any job in the last 2 years?

1. Yes 2. No 8. DK 9. NA

If NO, DK or NA go to Q.21

18. Have you had any jobs since (last) being made redundant?

1. Yes 2. No 8. DK

Go to Q.21

19. Did you retire early?

1. Yes 2. No 8. DK

If NO got to Q.21

20. Do you regret your decision to retire early?

1. Yes 2. No 8. DK

If YES could you tell me more about that please?

____

____

____

21. (a) What is your present (or your most recent) job?

____

(b) Are you (were you) in charge of others in this job?

1. Yes 2. No 3. Never had a job

Now I would like to ask just three questions about how your living standards have been affected recently.

22. Thinking about the amount of money coming into the household at the moment, which of the following applies most to you?

1. It is not possible to make ends meet.
2. We can just make ends meet
3. We manage quite well at the moment
4. None of these

NEW CARD

Identifier ☐

☐

☐

Card Number 2

23. I am going to read out a list of things most households have to spend money on. Could you tell me please whether, as a household, you are spending more, less or about the same on each item as at about this time last year?

Item	More	Less	Same	No Expenditure	DK	NA
Food/housekeeping	1	2	3	4	8	9
Fuel (eg. electricity/ gas)	1	2	3	4	8	9
Clothing and footwear for children	1	2	3	4	8	9
Clothing and footwear for you and other adults	1	2	3	4	8	9
Drinks	1	2	3	4	8	9
Tobacco	1	2	3	4	8	9
Things for the home (furnishings, appliances)	1	2	3	4	8	9
Savings	1	2	3	4	8	9
Holidays	1	2	3	4	8	9
Leisure and entertainment	1	2	3	4	8	9
Transport (fares, petrol)	1	2	3	4	8	9
Incidentals for the children	1	2	3	4	8	9

24. Would you mind telling me if you, or anyone in the household, receive any of the benefits listed on this card?

- State Retirement pension/old age pension ☐
- Private/Company pension ☐
- Widow's pension ☐
- Industrial Injury benefit or pension ☐
- Sickness or Invalidity benefit ☐
- Supplementary benefit ☐
- Unemployment benefit ☐
- Child Benefit/Family Allowance ☐
- Family income supplement (FIS) ☐
- Maternity allowance ☐

Attendance allowance ☐

Student/Retraining grant ☐

Mobility allowance ☐

Rent rebate/Rent allowance ☐

Rate rebate ☐

None of these ☐

And now some questions about how the job situation may be affecting people's health.

25. Thinking about the current job situation in Newport, how does it make you feel about your personal future and the future of others in your household (write in response): ______________________________

____

____

____

26. Would you say that the current job situation in Newport makes you feel: (read out list and probe for exact coding)

1. Very worried indeed.
2. Fairly worried.
3. Not worried

27. Has the current job situation in Newport affected your health in any way?

1. Yes 2. No (if No go to Q.29)

Could you tell me more about that please?

____

____

28. Have you spoken to anyone about this in the last 6 months?

1. No-one 2. Doctor 3. Relative

4. Friend 8. DK

29. Is there anything else that you would like to say about unemployment or its effects on you that we have not covered in the questions? (Does respondent believe that local people can actually do anything to improve the situation: probe as appropriate).

____

____

____

____

____

____

We don't want to pry, but we do need to know that we are getting a cross-section of the community, so:

30. Could you please tell me what your age is? Is it (read out):

1. 16-19	5. 35-39	9. 55-59
2. 20-24	6. 40-44	10. 60-64
3. 25-29	7. 45-49	11. 65+
4. 30-34	8. 50-54	12. DK

31. Sex of respondent.

1. Male 2. Female

32. Finally, I would like to briefly ask you about other adults in the household:

(a) Are there any other adults (16+)?

1. Yes 2. No

(b) How many adults are there? ☐

(c) Are there children (15 years and under)?

1. Yes 2. No

(d) How many children are there? ☐

NEW CARD Identifier ☐

☐

☐

Card number 3

33. Please fill in one column for each adult member ie. anybody 16 years and over, in the household.

	Adult 1	2	3	4	5	6	7
(a) Sex. 1. Male 2. Female							
Column	5	6	7	8	9	10	11
(b) What relation is this person to you? 1. Spouse/partner 2. Son/daughter 3. Sister/brother 4. Father/mother 5. Other relation 6. No relation							
Column	12	13	14	15	16	17	18
(c) Employment status. Is this person currently: (more than one category may be indicated) 1. In full-time employment 2. In part-time " 3. In casual " 4. Full-time housewife 5. Unemployed 6. Training 7. Retired 8. Ill/sick 9. Other ______________ A. DK							
Column	19 20	21 22	23 24	25 26	27 28	29 30	31 32
(d) If currently seeking work is she/he registered with any of the following: 1. Job Centre 2. Careers Office 3. PER 4. Not seeking work 5. None of these 6. DK							
Column	33	34	35	36	37	38	39
(e) Has this person been unemployed (ie. not in work but actively seeking a job) at any time in the last 2 years? 1. Yes 2. No 8.DK 9NA							
	40	41	42	43	44	45	46
(f) Has she/he been made redundant from any job in the last 2 years? 1. Yes 2. No 8.DK 9.NA							

contd.

Column	47	48	49	50	51	52	53

(g) Has he/she had any job since (last) being made redundant?
1. Yes 2. No 8.DK 9NA

Column	54	55	56	57	58	59	60

(h) What is this person's present or most recent job?

1. ____________ 2. ____________

3. ____________ 4. ____________

5. ____________ 6. ____________

7. ____________

Was he/she in charge of others at work?

1. Yes 8.DK
2. No 9.NA
3. Never had a job

Leave blank

Column	61	62	63	64	65	66	67

(i) What is her/his age?

1. 16-19 5. 35-39 9. 55-59
2. 20-24 6. 40-44 A. 60-64
3. 25-29 7. 45-49 B. 65+
4. 30-34 8. 50-54 C. DK

Column	70	71	72	73	74	75	76